just hold on
finding hope in the face of suicide

by Denise Haas, aka Big D

What is this book about?

I awoke this morning to yet another person who took her own life. She was a young girl. A teenager. I don't know why she did it, but I'm sure that in the midst of her anguish she believed the lie that there was no other option. I'm equally sure that the questions left in the minds of her friends and family will lead to grief beyond imagination. As a result of her suicide, some of those left behind will consider suicide themselves. Some will live a life that is barely living. Still some will go on to try to help others through their own nightmare of losing someone to suicide.

What do we say to someone who is suicidal? What can we possibly say to a Mom whose tears are permanently flowing because of the death of her son? How can we help a dad who weeps uncontrollably over the memory of his daughter even six years after that tragic day when his whole world was turned upside down? This book is not a cure-all, but I have no doubt in my mind that the things written in this book will help some, save others, and for many, prayerfully, this book will give them just enough hope to hold on.

I don't have a degree in psychology, and I won't pretend to know everything there is to know about suicide, but I will tell you that I've experienced it on a very personal level. Much of my teenage years were filled with contemplating suicide, which resulted in several attempts to take my own life. I've also interviewed several people for this book, and what they said can be used as an invaluable resource for even the most uninformed among us. If you're grieving the loss of a loved one, or you would just like to know what you can do in this fight against suicide, then this book would be a great place to start.

If you are considering suicide as a solution to the problems you are facing, I challenge you to continue reading. I've been right where you are, and what you are considering has grave (pun intended) and unintended consequences that you may not be aware of. Whenever we enter into an agreement, many times we are signing up for something we aren't expecting. It's called the fine print. I wrote this book to help you to see some of the "fine print" of your decision.

Thanks in advance for taking the time to read what I've written. I'm praying for you to see the truth.

Introduction & A Note to the Mental Health and Suicide Prevention Community

I know you care about people, especially those who are vulnerable to depression and suicide. Some of you have made suicide prevention your life's work, or at least a very large part of it. Your passion is to save lives.

To say that we don't understand the subject of suicide is an understatement. To say anyone understands it fully is to be completely deceived. We only know what we believe through the lens of our own personal experience and what we've been taught. Perhaps no exact solution will work for all people, because no two people are the same. However, since that's the case, I'm asking you to be open to what you read in this book. What worked for me may not work for others, but it just might work for someone, so that makes it worthwhile.

You may not agree with all of my conclusions. I only ask that you give this book a chance because it may actually help someone to choose life. I'm not pushing a religion, or promoting a certain church, but among other things, I am trying to open the door for those who are hurting to consider God as an alternative to suicide.

So, before you throw out the baby (this book) with the bath water (with its spiritual references), please consider that it might help **just** one person to choose life instead of death. Not everything written in this book is about God, but He's the only reason I'm alive today, so I must be truthful and not deny Him.

Whatever the case, as long as we keep our hearts right, sincere and not judgmental, our words will carry some amount of life and hope to everyone. Let's join together to do everything we possibly can to defeat this enemy of suicide, one life at a time using any and all tools at our disposal.

Thanks for not giving up on those who are struggling to *just hold on*.

Grateful Acknowledgments

There were two groups of people that I interviewed for this book: those who are grieving the loss of a loved one to suicide, and those who had attempted suicide. I'm extremely grateful to these who took valuable time out of their busy lives to do these interviews. I want to express my deepest thanks.

To the grieving: For all of you whose wounds have been unavoidably opened by this interviewing process, you have my eternal thanks.

To those who have attempted suicide: Your perspectives are invaluable, and will no doubt help those who don't understand the raw power and almost involuntary forward motion of a suicidal thought. Your insights will prove to be a ray of hope to some and an education to others. *Thank you.*

Together, these "interviewees" are my co-writers, so-to-speak. May you be rewarded in a thousand ways in your life and in the lives of many others because of your contribution to this book. (Look for the "interviewees" wisdom whenever you see, "**From the Interviews**.")

A note of thanks to my editor, Martha DiPalma

It's not easy to "fine tune" another person's creative work. It takes finesse, patience, and a certain amount of sensitivity to work with the sensitivities of a writer. Somehow, time and time again, Martha has continued to find that balance with me. I didn't take all of her advice, so please don't judge her editing abilities by this book alone. If there are grammatical errors, or sentence structures that don't seem too structurally sound, that's on me. There were certain things I just wouldn't bend on, rules of English notwithstanding. Even beyond the editing though, Martha is my mentor, friend and sister in Christ.

May the Lord bless you, Martha, for doing what He has called you to do in His Kingdom. With all of the thousands of lives you've already touched, I don't think you've even scratched the surface of the amazing ways God is going to use you in the future! *Shalom, dear sister, and thank you.*

Thank *you* for your support

I'm extremely grateful to those who have contributed to this book both financially and spiritually, through prayer. Because anonymity is often a characteristic of humble people, I know you wouldn't want me to name you, but you know who you are. It's quite obvious to me that I couldn't have finished this work without your support. *Thank YOU.*

A shout out to my husband, Curt

Through your wisdom and patience, you have helped to make my first book writing experience a pleasant one. I can't thank you enough for your support. Life with you just keeps getting better and better. *I love you, and goodnight.*

Of course, I also want to acknowledge and thank Jesus for His clear leading in this entire writing process. Writing a book can be a daunting prospect, but I have felt God's hand guiding me every step of the way. There are few things in my life that I've been completely sure that the Lord was leading, and this book is one of those things. For that reason alone, I know God will speak to people through it, and many who are weary will have an encounter with their Creator because of it. The idea that God would use me (the "foolish things of this world, and the base things and the despised" 1 Corinthians 1:27) to bring glory to His name through a book is both humbling and exciting at the same time. I'm grateful that so many years ago Jesus rescued me, and now my story has become His-story. I am fully His for the fullness of time and eternity. I thank Jesus for this work, and leave the results of this book to Him.

This book is dedicated to the weary ones.
May the words on these pages sustain you to
just hold on.
"The Lord GOD has given Me the tongue of disciples,
that I may know how to sustain the
weary one with a word...." **Isaiah 50:4**

Table of Contents

Part One

To Those Who Are
Contemplating Suicide

I f you're contemplating suicide today, this book is for
you. If you feel like you've already made up your
mind, please keep reading. Some say that suicide is a
selfish and cowardly act, but I disagree. If you've picked
up this book, then I believe there is a strength in you that
calls you to live, and you are meant to read it. Be courageous and read the whole thing.

If you read this entire book and end up with questions or doubts about your initial choice to take your life,
please email me: dhaasbigd@gmail.com. I will respond
as quickly as is humanly possible.

Don't make a permanent decision based on temporary feelings, even if you've had those feelings for years.
YOU are the reason I have written this book. **YOU** are
valuable and worth every effort that it took for me to

get these truths down on paper. No matter what you've done-let me say that again-no matter what you've done or haven't done, **YOU** have not gone too far.

As long as you're breathing, there is hope for you. *Just hold on for one more second, just one more minute, just one more hour. Just hold on for one more sunrise, one more time to open your eyes to blue skies and hope and love and the warmth of the sun. Just let your lungs keep breathing... and please, just hold on.*

We begin with **Five Really Good Reasons NOT to Take Your Own Life**

Really Good Reason Not to Take Your Own Life #1: *Collateral Damage (People)*

It's extremely interesting to me that the people that I interviewed who had attempted suicide, said that they were not thinking about what their death would do to their family and friends. Only one person said that she was glad she didn't succeed because that would have devastated her children. She wrote, *"They would have never recovered from my suicide."*

On the other hand, one hundred percent of the grieving people that I interviewed were devastated by the death of their loved one. Some are still grieving several years after that horrific event.

If you've not thought of it before, here is an example of what your suicide will do to your family, friends and even complete strangers. The following portrayal is from the perspective of a grown woman whose older brother committed suicide when she was seven years old.

(Dear reader: The following is a very harsh piece of writing intended to reach those who are contemplating suicide right now. If you are grieving the loss of a loved one to suicide, please skip "Suicide Ruined My Life.")

Suicide Ruined My Life

"The day you left was a day I will never forget. It's with me wherever I go, and I can't escape it, the day you left. I don't sleep much, I'm not very hungry, just sort of exist from day to day because the day is always the same, it's the day you left. I feel so empty except for the guilt that fills me up.

People tell me all the time that *Time* will heal this pain, but I don't see how. When I close my eyes, I see you ending your life. I see your face and I wonder, 'Did you think about me at all on the day you threw your life away?' Every time I see new life, a flower, or hear a baby cry, I'm reminded that you are not alive, and you never will be again.

The day you threw your life away left a permanent and deep scar on my life and on the way I look at things.

My life is filled with questions now that I never would've thought about before that day. I'm lost and alone and hurt by your decision to throw your life away. I'm never sure of myself or confident in any relationships that I have.

The day you went to the grave, you took with you my innocence and trust and in return gave me confusion, anger and bitterness. I always looked up to you, thought I knew you, thought you loved me, but then, without even saying goodbye, you were gone. Gone forever.

Your decision to end your life has very much redefined mine. I have only this tragedy to remember you by as it replays in my mind day after day.

I've had years of therapy and drugs to help with my 'illness' that I got the day you left, but nothing seems to help. I can't seem to make sense of it. Did you even think of what your suicide would do to a seven year old? Why did you do it? It's the question that haunts my mind all my waking hours. I miss you so much.

Even after these many years, I'm still reliving the guilt of not being there for you. I know I was only your 'little sister,' but you didn't even give me the chance to help.

So, how is it being dead? Is it better? Are you happy? Was it worth it, that day you threw your life (and mine) away? I hope so, because it sure didn't help me any, I won't ever be happy. I will always remember the day you threw your life away because I can't escape it. I can't get free of it. It won't let me go. **Suicide ruined my life and I'll never be the same.**" dh

If you're considering suicide, I beg you to think of those you will leave behind, the collateral damage, if you will: I'm your brother, your mother, your best friend, your teacher, sister, Grandma, husband, your next door neighbor, your niece, your son. We're the ones you will leave behind to pick up the pieces.

If you're successful, you will put us in an impossible position; no one will be comforted, there won't be any words to describe the constant ache in the deepest part of our being. We won't be able to explain it to the kids, we'll keep it to ourselves, but we will be in agony everyday wondering if we could've said or done anything differently.

You will leave us with a new sort of "self-condemnation" by which we will filter some of our decisions. We all love you; can't you see that? Do you really want to leave us with an agonizing, guilt-ridden memory of your suicide? If suicide takes your life, be assured that it will ruin our lives too.

Have you considered that the children might follow your example to the grave? In your pain, you think you're doing us a favor, but your death will have the exact opposite effect on our lives. Make no mistake. Your suicide will ruin our lives, and we'll never be the same.

Please, just hold on for one more second, just one more minute, just one more hour...

*From the Interviews
Think YOU don't matter? The following statements were gathered from the interviews I conducted with those who are grieving the loss of a loved one to suicide.

A Life Of Grief: In Their Own Words: *"Because just surviving is a far cry from living"* dh

Here was the question I asked those who grieve the loss of a loved one to suicide: *"If you could say anything to your loved one, what would it be?"*

"Why?" Helen (lost her son)

"I would holler at them, why did you do this to me?" Geri (lost two of her sons to suicide in a span of five years)

"I wish that in the last moments of your life on this earth you would have seen the impact of your actions on all who loved you. I believe that if you had a moment of clarity through your pain, addictions and anger—you would have made a very different series of decisions that day. I know that you know just how much I loved you—and that my efforts to hold you

accountable for your actions were part of my love."
Toni (lost her brother)

"**I love you.**" Carol (lost her son)

"**I'm sorry.**" April (lost her son)

"**I miss you, but I know you're not hurting anymore.**"
Pat (lost his sister)

"**I'm sorry. I didn't know things were so bad for you.**"
Sue (lost her son)

"**I love you and I miss you.**" Carrie (lost her sister)

"**I didn't want you to go. We would have had a tough
time, but we could have gotten through it together.**"
Kim (lost her husband)

*From the Interviews
Below are statements from the people who have lost
a loved one to suicide, in answer to my question, "*If
someone was standing before you right now saying
they wanted to take their own life, what would you say
to them?*"

If YOU are contemplating suicide, here's what the grieving families are saying directly to you in their own words:

"Don't do it! You really don't want to die, do you? You just want the pain to stop. I can help you stop it."

"No one is better off without you, just ask Mom."

"It's temporary at this moment. Life is full of pain, but we get through it."

"Don't even think about it. Please don't!"

"You can't. You just can't do this to your family. They will never be the same. So many people care about you! People love you!"

"Please, let's talk about this. Why? There is a way out! Please, we can find a solution-think about your family."

"The only hope you have is Jesus. He can be your life. Only Jesus can lift you out of your darkness."

Really Good Reason Not to Take Your Own Life #2:
There are worse things than dying

Living With the Consequences of Attempted Suicide

Not everyone who attempts suicide will succeed. According to some studies, *approximately 92-95% of attempts will end in survival.* [1]

Survival doesn't mean there are no consequences. Quite the contrary, the attempt may not take your life, but it can definitely compromise the quality of your remaining life.

I have heard stories of people who have attempted suicide through heinous means and have not succeeded in dying. For example, there are stories of men and women who have jumped off bridges, but did not die. Instead they are paralyzed and must be cared for the rest of their days on this earth. There are those who have tried to shoot themselves who now have to live with deformities and endure painful surgeries. There are those who have taken poisons and are now brain damaged with the inability to speak, walk or reason.

Now, all of these methods may have worked for others, but by God's sovereign will, they did not succeed in those whose time was not yet up. Still, in these cases, the unsuccessful suicide attempt has irrevocably altered life as they know it.

Surviving the attempt

According to one source, The Skyway Bridge in St. Petersburg, Florida, is one of the most used bridges for suicide in the Nation. *People who make the jump hit the water in approximately 3.5 seconds going about 75 mph. The impact typically breaks bones and ruptures organs. Even if the impact doesn't kill them, people are knocked unconscious and drown.* [2]

Over the last decade, the Tampa Bay Times has interviewed two people who survived the jump. **Both said they regretted the decision to jump just before they hit the water.** The impact was so violent that it ripped off their clothes.

One survivor, whose bowels were ruptured and back broken, described the feeling like crashing through a wooden deck. A nearby boater rescued her. The other survivor suffered a collapsed lung, broken ribs, ruptured spleen and a fractured vertebra in his neck. He swam to nearby rocks and was rescued.

So, we see that there really are worse things than dying. Ultimately, all life is in God's hands. He wants you to live, and so do I. Please don't try to take your life. *Just hold on… the sun will shine again for you. It did for me.*

Really Good Reason Not to Take Your Own Life #3:
You are worth it and you matter

One of the prevailing thoughts in the mind of a depressed or suicidal person is the idea that they are worth-LESS. In my interviews with the people who attempted suicide, worthlessness was a consistent theme that ran through their lives.

If I were to ask you right now what you think you are worth, what would you say? "Not much," "A little," "That depends on who you ask," "I don't really know," etc. The problem with those kinds of answers is that they are usually, if not always, based upon the opinion and valuation of another person.

Here's the thing. Every human being, male and female, was made in the image of God **(Genesis 1:27)**. For that reason alone, each one of us has intrinsic value.

The Bible says in **Ephesians, chapter 2, verse 10** that we are His (God's) *workmanship.* Another version says that we are His *masterpiece.* You may not feel like it, look like it, or act like an invaluable masterpiece of God, but true is true, you are. So, even if no one on the earth loved you (and that just isn't possible. Someone loves you), you would still be worth every effort that God made to save you.

You may have heard that old saying, "God don't make no junk," and that is so right. Our value as human beings

29

is not based on how much money we make or how good looking we are, where we live, how well we can sing, dance, paint, or write, or what anyone has said about us. **No.** Our worth is set in stone to be at the highest valuation because of Whose image we were made in. You can't get more valuable than being made in the image of God for the purpose of God.

*From the Interviews
Here is some advice from those who have **attempted suicide**. Please take it to heart. These people have been right where you are. The question I asked them was, *"If someone was standing before you right now saying they wanted to take their own life, what would you say to them?"*

"You're beautiful and you're one-of-a-kind. God has a purpose for you, and your life is not an accident." Christina, Author / Musician / Minister

"Let's talk. Hold on one more day. Stay with me." Brian, Minister

"It really does get better. I know you can't see past this moment. I will sit with you. I will stay with you." Mary, High School Teacher

"Tomorrow will be better. Keep saying it until it happens." Lauren

No Matter What, You Matter

So, I'll ask you again, what are you worth? If your answer is based on God's view of you then you've hit the nail on the head.

No matter what anyone has said to you, no matter how much you've been kicked around or made fun of, no matter how many times you've failed, or sinned, or tried to do better, no matter what evil you have seen, or lies you have heard, no matter what you've come to believe, you will never be WORTH LESS than what God has made you to be. You are nothing less than God's masterpiece, and YOU MATTER!

Jesus is speaking, *"For this reason I say to you, do not be worried about your life, as to what you will eat or what you will drink; nor for your body, as to what you will put on. Is not life more than food, and the body more than clothing? Look at the birds of the air, that they do not sow, nor reap nor gather into barns, and yet your heavenly Father feeds them. Are you not worth much more than they? And who of you by being worried can add a single hour to his life?"* (Matthew 6:25-27)

Understanding your worth to God is a tangible truth that can help you to *just hold on*.

Really Good Reason Not to Take Your Own Life #4:
Suicide is Contagious

It's a horrifying thing to think that your 4 year old little brother or sister would grow up wanting to be just like their big brother who took his life.

As humans, we are prone to suggestion. Suggestion can be so compelling that we actually have a phrase for it, "the power of suggestion." Advertisers know it works and they use the power of suggestion to sell their products. But even advertisers know that the personal recommendation of another (word of mouth) is the most effective way to get people to buy what they're selling. Every day we are leading and suggesting through our words and our actions.

Here's a lighthearted (sweet) story that gets my point across on a very basic level.

The POWER of Suggestion

Just the other day I was driving to Walmart. First, a little background. After like 35 years of eating very unhealthily, I have turned over a new leaf in the past few months. I have been on a self-imposed, customized "live-it" (not die-t); composed of carrot juice, meat, fruit and vegetables. As a practice, I try not to eat bread, chips, candy bars, or fast food anymore.

Ok, back to the sweet story. So, there I was waiting to make my turn onto the highway when this guy turned onto the street right in front of me. He was a stranger, but what he was doing would drive me to go off the reservation, *food wise*, that is.

As he made his turn, time slowed down long enough for me to see that he was eating an ice cream cone from Dairy Queen. The moment was like one of those model commercials where their hair is blowing in the breeze and everything is in slow motion. It was a split second glance and I was toast.

"Oh," I said to myself out loud, "I **WILL** get an ice cream cone on my way home today."

There's so much power in suggestion that I'm almost positive that if you're still reading this, you are also going to get an ice cream cone this very day. I apologize if I have ruined your diet; it was not my intention. However, I pretty much knew if I wrote down my experience, you would be sucked into my world.

No doubt as I drove home that day, eating my chocolate cone, and making my turn into that same street, someone else was watching ME (I looked like a model with my hair blowing in the breeze), and boom, another customer for Dairy Queen.

Now, I'm not trying to make light of your situation, I'm just showing you that if our example has that much power in the little things like an ice cream cone, how much more power will it have on these matters of life and death? I'm telling you suicide is contagious. You don't want to spread that disease, do you? I know you don't. Besides, if bad life choices are contagious, then so could your choice to *just hold on* become a real *life-saver* to someone else.

Really Good Reason Not to Take Your Own Life # 5:
Hell is a real place.

Have you considered the reality of Hell?
To be honest, I really don't know if a person who commits suicide will go to hell. I only know that I had a fear of going there when I was contemplating suicide back in my teenage days. That fear of going to Hell actually helped me for many years not to make a serious attempt at taking my own life. I think that since it is such a serious question, and nobody has a definitive answer on it, we should probably NOT test it out. So, please *just hold on*, because eternity is a very long time.

Now you may be thinking, "Those five reasons not to take my own life were pretty good, BUT what do I do with all of this depression?" Well, let's talk about why you could be depressed in the first place.

Cause, Effect, and Real Life Solutions

This section is chock-full of opinions. It is not intended to be a clinical assessment, medical advice or college level psychology. This is just me sharing opinions that have been born out raw life experience, common sense, and real life solutions that have worked for me. I apologize in advance if I make you angry. It is certainly not my intention, but for some it will be an unavoidable result. Keep reading!

If, as many say, depression is to blame for suicide, then the causes of depression should be explored. In this next section, we will consider some of the possible reasons for depression, and we will also consider real-life solutions to the problems of anxiety and depression.

WHY Am I Depressed? HELP!
Could the cause of this depression be physical?

Poor Nutrition/FOOD

I've learned (only recently) that our psyche is seriously affected by deficiencies in nutrition. I don't mean that our first choice should be to pop a Flintstone vitamin to fix that problem, but more like eat some meat for your brain, or eat five apples for energy or whatever. What if various nutritious foods could relieve some of your depression? I mean it's worth the time to look at the possibility, right?

Lack of SLEEP

Sleep is the coolest thing ever when you think about it. God has placed an automatic shut down on the human body after a specific period of time every day. Our bodies will be in charging mode for 6-8 hours in order to reboot our brains and bodies. God is effectively putting us to sleep every night for our own good. Isn't that amazing? Because these bodies were made to need sleep, when we don't get enough of it, we start to short circuit. Not getting enough rest can be a real downer.

Your poor sleep patterns might be the culprit for physical exhaustion and a lack of motivation. Think about the melt down your cell phone has if you don't charge it. It gets all crazy for a time, beeping and vibrating to warn you of imminent shut down. If you try to ignore those warnings, the phone will eventually shut itself down. The only way to turn it back on is to charge it.

It's the same thing with our brains. Being the complicated computers that they are, they need to be recharged every day in order to function properly. Take a nap or go to bed early. Hey, it might help.

Lack of Water

I haven't always respected water, but as I've seen the serious effects of dehydration, I can appreciate the role that water plays in our physical and mental health. I'm sure you know this, but human beings are made up of 60% water. Some of the symptoms of dehydration are: irritability, confusion, tiredness, low blood pressure, and sunken eyes. In severe cases, dehydration can cause delirium or unconsciousness.

On the other hand, the benefits of water are fabulous! Among many other things, *water in the human body acts as a shock absorber for the spinal cord and brain, and lubricates joints. The brain also uses water to manufacture hormones and neurotransmitters, and water helps to deliver oxygen all over the body.* [5] You do see how a lack of water will greatly compromise our mental health, right? Your depression could be caused, at least in part, by a lack of water. Easy fix. Come to think of it, I'm kind of thirsty and a little bit confused at the moment. I think I'll go get a glass of water.

We see this (food, sleep, and water) scenario played out in the life of the prophet Elijah. After God had used him in a great way, Elijah got depressed. Guess what the prophet of God wanted to do? Die. Yup. He said, *"It is enough; now, O Lord, take my life, for I am not better than my fathers."* (**1 Kings 19:4**) Classic honest, human talk right there.

What was the solution for Elijah? The angel brought him some food and water, and then God put him to sleep for a while. This happened twice. Then, Elijah woke up refreshed and ready to serve the Lord again. You can read the whole story in the Bible in **1 Kings 19:4-14.**

Lack of Exercise

I'm told that exercise is one of the three things that makes our serotonin levels higher. Serotonin is one of the chemicals in our body that makes us "feel" good emotionally. According to this study from the National Institute for Health and Clinical Excellence, *"...there are two mechanisms by which physical activity increases brain serotonin. First, motor activity increases the rate and frequency at which serotonin is 'fired' within the brain, resulting in an increase in both the release and synthesis of it. Secondly, regular exercise increases the level of tryptophan in the brain (an amino acid used to manufacture serotonin). The exact mechanism is not clearly understood; however, **it is clear that aerobic exercise improves mood through increasing brain serotonin levels.**"* [8]

Even beyond all of that fancy research, don't we all feel better after we exercise? I know I do. The point is, exercise plays a definite role in contributing to a healthy, happy mind.

Thyroid

I've actually had friends who have told me, after extensive testing, that the reason they were always tired, unmotivated, gaining weight, and depressed was because their thyroid was out of whack. Two scenarios could occur if your thyroid gland is not functioning correctly: hypothyroidism and hyperthyroidism.

Here are just a few of the symptoms of **hypothy-roidism**: Trouble sleeping, tiredness and fatigue, difficulty concentrating, dry skin and hair, and depression. And here are some of the symptoms for **hyperthy-roidism**: Anxiety, irritability or moodiness, nervousness, and hyperactivity. [9]

We can see that the thyroid gland can cause some real and present mental issues in a person's everyday life. If you are having some of these problems, it might be a good idea to go to the doctor and get your thyroid checked.

And while we're on the subject of chemicals in the body that can wreak havoc in the mind, let's not underestimate the power of a hormonal imbalance. The struggle is real. Personal note: For years, I have sought for a solution to my P.M.S. (I'm talking about the mental and emotional aspect of P.M.S., not the physical aspect). After much searching, I finally found a natural solution that works for me. During certain times of the month, I rub some Lavender essential oil (in full strength) onto the bottom of my feet. (Warning: This oil is very strong so I don't suggest you put it anywhere else on your skin as it may cause a rash.) I didn't use to believe that essential oils were all that essential until they worked for me. Wow, what a difference! If our hormone levels are out of balance (without the thyroid being to blame), then we need to find the solution (preferably through natural methods such as foods, essential oils, etc.) that can boost those specific hormones that we are lacking. Is it possible that some of the diagnosis for mental illness is really just a serious hormone imbalance or a thyroid issue? It's just a thought.

Could This Depression Be Caused By Physical Pain?

In my research and interviews, I have found that some people who want to take their own lives are those who are just worn down by constant pain in their body. They've been in an accident, or have become sick, or some other thing is causing daily, excruciating physical pain. They try to get relief through pain medication prescribed by their doctor. Despite the pain medication, this brutal pain lingers day after day.

As the pain tolerance to the medication grows higher, the pain meds don't even begin to touch the pain, so they need more. Addiction begins to set in. These people who were previously mentally sound (before the accident or sickness) are now addicts.

￢lization in itself can cause major depression.
ind progressive cycle that they are trying
their own. Because of embarrassment and

shame at the question of "how did I get here?" the person hides the problem. With no one to talk to (by their own choice), they become isolated and alone. The person can then start to feel like they are a burden to their family and to those who care for them. The next thing you know, they are considering a permanent way out.

I can totally see how this happens, but suicide is not a reasonable option in this or any situation.

Family and friends are there to help. Tell one of them how desperate you have become. I can almost guarantee that they will go into "solution mode" and do whatever they can to help you get through this. It's imperative that you tell one of your caregivers what you are going through. They love you and they will walk through any valley with you, but you have to tell them what's happening. By communicating with others, you will know you are not alone and this will bring a ray of light into the darkness of addiction.

I bet if we really knew the truth, there would be a lot of people in your same predicament. If those in this situation could only tell someone, I know they would find tangible help.

Could the Cause Of This Depression Be My Use of Illegal Drugs?

Here's another kind of no-brainer when it comes to a possible cause of depression: the use of meth, cocaine, heroin… all of these will mess with your mental health. I'm sure you agree. If you are doing these drugs, get some help, please. The end of this road is not pretty or happy in any way. Would I be right in assuming that you've tried to help yourself more than once, but have failed every time?

You're not a terrible person because you are addicted to these drugs. Like every single human being, you're just in need of reconciliation with your Maker. Addiction is a wicked slave master, and the only way out of this bondage is through calling upon your Creator, God.

You are a valuable creation of God. You are not a lost cause. You can be useful to your family, friends and society once again, but you need to get up and try to break this cycle of addiction. Call out to God in your desperation. He will hear you, and He wants to help you. Then, allow Him to lead you to people that He has ordained to help you. Call someone whom you know has beat this already, or call a Christian friend or Minister that you can trust.

I know it's hard to reach out, but freedom is next to impossible on your own. And when people come to help you, don't refuse their help. Could it be that God sent them in response to your prayer? You are worth every effort. *Just hold on.*

Could the Cause Of This Depression Be Side Effects From LEGAL Drugs?
Prescribed Medication

Then there's the old "side effects of prescription drugs" dilemma. Sure, sometimes we're on the wrong blood pressure medicine, or too much of something, or one drug may be reacting with another drug we're taking. There are so many reasons why someone may be depressed because of prescription drugs that we would be here for twenty-five days trying to cover them. Every **BODY** is different.

Have a personal conversation with your doctor. What works for someone else may not be working for you. It's your life, so do some research, and don't be intimidated or afraid to make suggestions. Make sure your doctor understands that the possible side effects are ruining your mental stability. Good doctors want to help. That's why many of them became doctors in the first place. Try to work together to find a solution. Your mental health could depend on it.

Could the Cause of This Depression Be Psychological?
Psychological/Emotional

Have you had a tragedy occur in your life recently? Such as a death in the family, a breakup of a relationship, or a physical limitation caused by an accident? I think we can all agree that life is hard, and those events listed above can be real reasons for grief and sadness, for sure.

Depression isn't always "mysterious" or "for no reason." Many times, something has actually happened that has altered a person's life in such a way that they get sad, and will even get to the point of despairing of life.

Sometimes it's helpful to figure out how you personally tick to determine what triggers are contributing to your present depression or anxiety. This is actually normal for human beings. God made us with feelings and emotions. If someone doesn't react with sadness to a sad event (someone who has no conscience—no empathy), I think we call them a psychopath.

The thing is, we were created to grieve, to be sad, to get angry, to be happy, to be excited, etc. The problem comes in when these emotions start to control us. Is it possible that we have never learned to find our way out of these emotions that were caused by the tragedy and that we're living in a "mysterious depression" today because of it?

A word about **psychological drugs:**

Since there is no actual test to measure anything inside your mind (only the chemicals in the brain), when it comes to wholly man-made drugs to treat the mind, we should be very careful. We know some of these psychological drugs can cause terrible and undesirable side effects that are, ironically, the exact thing we are trying to prevent, i.e. anxiety, depression and suicide. If the side effect of a drug is suicidal thoughts, should we really take it?

In my opinion, these psych drugs should be used sparingly and as a last resort. In rare cases, perhaps these drugs *can* help people, especially in the short term, to get through an immediate crisis. Of course, I am not a doctor (nor do I play one on TV), but in my interviews of those who had lost a loved one to suicide, about seventy percent of the people who took their lives were on anti-depressants, anti-psychotics, or anti-anxiety medication.

I'm not saying the medication was seventy percent to blame, but my findings are interesting. With such a high failure rate, wouldn't we want to be a little *more cautious* in our dispensing of such drugs? (I am not suggesting that anyone should go off his or her meds "cold turkey." I am suggesting, however, that people who are on these medications consider alternative options slowly. As mentioned earlier, there may be other causes for the depression/anxiety and also less drastic treatments available).

Could This Depression Be Caused By Grief? (See Part Two: To the Grieving)

Could the Cause of This Depression Be Ongoing Abuse?

If you are being abused, please find a way to tell someone. It seems to me that a common element in any case of abuse is intimidation. The threats of bodily harm by your abuser (to you or to those you love) are lies designed to silence you. As long as you are silent about being abused, the abuser is protected from being exposed. This pain you are experiencing could be the cause of depression. Please involve someone so that you can receive help.

Could the Cause Of This Depression Be Historical?

What? Ok, let me explain that one. Many folks I interviewed for this book who have attempted suicide have had horrendous childhoods. They have been abused (in every way imaginable), abandoned, unwanted, defenseless, and confused in a plethora of ways as children. Maybe you have been, too.

Some people have had a great childhood, but will end up in abusive relationships, be violated, or witness a terrible event as adults. All of these experiences have the potential to leave a lasting residue on a person, which can manifest as anger, insecurity, fear, distrust, unfaithfulness, unforgiveness, bitterness, and more.

The psychological community has labeled these as various disorders. They are right. There are disorders, but genuine healing does exist through true forgiveness. It begins when the offended person releases the offender, at least in his or her mind. Letting the criminal go (in our minds), sets *us* free to live life without the residue of the past, which can manifest itself as mental illness in the future.

I know that forgiving a person who has abused you flies in the face of all logic and justice, but it does work. It's not easy, but forgiving others is an effective means of bringing real, emotional healing to the one who forgives.

Depression and Torment As a Result of Not Forgiving Others

There's a story that Jesus told in **Matthew 18** about a King who had forgiven one of his servants millions of dollars. Because the servant had no way of repaying his debt to the King, he fell on his knees and begged the King to have patience with him until he could repay the debt. He wasn't asking for forgiveness of the entire amount he owed, just some time to pay it (it would have taken him about **200,000 years** to pay his debt—impossible!). Amazingly, the King felt compassion and forgave him the entire debt!

What do you think the newly forgiven servant did after receiving such a great gift? Well, he immediately went out and found one of his fellow servants who owed HIM a few thousand dollars. He yelled at him, "Pay me back what you owe me or I will throw you into jail!" The fellow servant fell down before him and begged him to give him some time to pay (it would have taken him about **a hundred days** to pay him back). The wicked servant began to choke him, got the cops and had the guy thrown into jail!

When the King heard the story, he was furious and this is what he said, *"'You wicked slave, I forgave you all that debt because you pleaded with me. Should you not also have had mercy on your fellow slave, in the same way that I had mercy on you?'* **And his lord, moved with anger, handed him over to the torturers until he should repay all that was owed him. Jesus said, *'My heavenly Father will also do the same to you, if each of you does not forgive his brother from your heart.'"* (Matthew 18:32-35)**

What? A loving God will turn us over to the torturers if we don't forgive others? Did I read that right? Yup. The consequence of unforgiveness will feel like torture to us. It will not only affect our minds through constant anxiety, but it can begin to eat away at our bodies causing all manner of physical dysfunction.

You see, in God's Kingdom it's literally impossible to repay what God has done for us. Because God has forgiven us a debt that we could never pay (not in a million years), how dare we go out and demand ANY DEBT be repaid to us! Forgiveness is the key here. Once we experience it from God, we should be more apt to forgive others' sins against us, no matter how bad they are.

However, if you haven't yet asked the "King" (God) to forgive you, you should do that first. Without His forgiveness, it's not even possible to forgive others.

Now, you may be asking, "Could this depression that I'm experiencing today be caused by something in my past that I have not forgiven someone for?" It sure can.

A few more things about forgiveness: it's not as complicated or as hard as we sometimes make it. Part of forgiving is accepting the fact that people who don't know God don't know what they are doing. Jesus said this while He was on the cross, *"Forgive them Father for they know not what they do."* **(Luke 23:24)**

Forgiveness is also **not forgetting** what's been done to us. It's just letting go of the offenders in our minds and hearts, with the understanding that God is the ultimate, righteous judge Who will settle that account with them on our behalf. Forgiveness is just transferring our right to judge (because of a wrong done to us) into the very capable hands of the only **ONE** Who can give them exactly what they deserve. In the meantime, through forgiving those who have hurt us, we are setting ourselves free from the tormentors. You might want to try this, and see if it works.

Those Lies That Keep Replaying In My Head...

Every single one of the people I interviewed who had attempted suicide said they felt worth less because a teacher, a parent, a peer, a sibling, and even church people had said horrible things to them. Things like, *"You'll never amount to anything,"* and *"You're a loser, nobody wants you around,"* and even, *"Why don't you just die? The world would be a better place without you."*

Do you feel the power in those words? (I even hesitated to write them.) Maybe you've heard them. Maybe you've said them. Either way, those evil declarations are seeds that grow up to become trees of despair, rage and death, and they come straight from the devil himself. It's highly possible that those lies could be the cause of the depression you are now experiencing. Destroy them by giving them to Jesus, and then replace them with truthful, life-giving phrases.

Speak Life

Some of us may be depressed or obsessed with death because we're allowing those phrases to play and replay in our minds. Words have power. The Bible says, *"Death and life are in the power of the tongue, and those who love it will eat its fruit."* **(Proverbs 18:21)** So, you see that the wisest man in the world (Solomon who penned Proverbs) makes it clear. We all need to heed this truth. When we speak to our kids, our friends, family or complete strangers, let's speak life. Do you think the world would be a happier, healthier place if we did?

Could the Cause of This Depression Be a Secret Sin?

If you've sinned, don't keep it in!

Sometimes people are doing something wrong but no one on the earth knows about it. They are so filled with shame that they can't tell anyone. This "secret sin" will eventually eat a person alive.

When I was a child, I did something wrong. I didn't tell anyone because I knew I would get into trouble. That secret sin ended up ruining a good portion of the next few months of my young life. Out of that experience was born my very first thought of suicide. I simply could not see another way out.

The right solution? The solution is to confess that secret. I suppose that's why people go to counselors and psychologists, or even priests. But you don't have to go to a professional to confess a sin. Through His death on the cross, Jesus made it possible for us to go straight to God.

Even people in the Bible were guilty of secret sin. Through a series of sins and cover-ups, David, the King of Israel, committed adultery and murder. It was a secret to people, but no sin is hidden from God.

Here's what King David had to say about holding on to secret sin: *"When I kept silent about my sin, my body wasted away through my groaning all day long. For day and night Your hand was heavy upon me; my vitality was drained away as with the fever heat of summer."* Do you see depression described here? It sucks the life right out of a person and it actually has adverse effects on the physical body as well as the mind. **(Psalm 32:3-4)**

But look what happened after he confessed his sin to God. *"I acknowledged my sin to You, and my iniquity I did not hide; I said, 'I will confess my transgressions to the LORD'; And You forgave the guilt of my sin."*

Wow! Do you see how hiding sin brings depression, but confessing it brings forgiveness and freedom?

King David goes on to serve the Lord faithfully for the rest of his life. We have a great treasure in the

Book of Psalms that David wrote out of His relationship with God.

There's also a time to confess our sins to other people after we confess to God. This confession of our sins to one another, we are told in **James 5:16**, will bring healing to the offender.

Could the cause of this depression be "PETernal"?

Ha-ha, now I'm just making stuff up. I used to say, *"Well, I'm not maternal because I'm not great with kids, but I love my pets. I guess that makes me PETernal."*

Have you considered getting a dog? Prison can be a place where a person could lose all hope, especially if someone has a life sentence. But even behind bars, prisoners are finding joy again. There are experimental programs that bring rescue dogs into the prisons so that they can be trained by the prisoners. *"Behind the walls of correctional institutions, inmates find a renewed sense of purpose through working with injured and rescued animals."* [3]

These pet training programs are working. They are restoring a sense of humanity to the most violent of criminals. These people are learning to be gentle again-to exercise love and to care for something that cannot care for itself. These "throwaways" of society have a purpose again. These broken and damaged human beings are being rehabilitated in the process of caring for these unwanted and abandoned animals.

God made pets for us to enjoy. I also think He may have given them to us for our healing. Animals can produce real-life mental health in the lives of hurting and happy people alike.

Could This Depression Be Caused, At Least In Part, By The Company I Keep?

We've all been around negative people, complaining about everything under the sun, ungrateful, and often speaking badly about other people. They're like Winnie-the-Pooh's sidekick, Eeyore. Like some kind of mental anchor, they can drag us down.

I'm not saying you should abandon your negative friends, just maybe taper off a little on the time you spend in their presence. It might help you not to be negative, anxious, or even depressed. On the other hand, if YOU are the negative one, may I suggest you try to change?

There's an old hymn that goes like this: *"Count your blessings, name them one by one…."* No matter how bad we think we may have it, there's always something to be thankful for, right? Counting our blessings can actually lead to less negativity, which could result in less depression. A thankful person is a happy person. Try speaking your blessings out loud. As we saw earlier in regard to our words, it behooves us to speak positively, if only because we will end up "eating our words." [… *those who love it* (the tongue) *will eat its fruit* (words). **Proverbs 18:21**]

The company I'm talking about is not just the flesh and blood people we hang around with, it's also the ideas on the radio, TV, music, websites, and other things that we fill our time and minds with. I've cut down immensely on the time I spend watching TV because it just wasn't helping me. If we want to be happy, we have to start surrounding ourselves with those things that are good for us.

Speaking of Music

Music can either be a great help to our mental health or it can be a tool to gravely compromise it. When I was a teenager, music was one of the most powerful influences in my life. I would listen to the saddest songs I could find and wonder why I was so sad.

Some people say that they don't listen to the words in songs, they only listen because they like the music. Don't be deceived. If you're listening to the music, the lyrics are being planted in your heart at the same time. Those seeds (words) will produce fruit. It may take a while, but what we listen to, watch and allow into our minds will shape us into its own image.

Music Can Be Influential

Case in point, my love for America. No one in my family has ever been engaged in active combat, yet I have this overwhelming love for this country and for the soldiers who fight for Her. Why am I so patriotic? I wondered. After some thought, I traced my patriotism back to my days in the fourth grade. It was 1976, bicentennial year. That year in school, we learned just about every patriotic song about America that was ever written. At the end of the year, we put on a musical program to celebrate America's 200th anniversary. Is it possible that musical experience could have influenced my patriotism? I'm pretty sure it did.

Music Can Be a Powerful Anti-Depressant

The day I met Jesus was the day I started to listen to Christian music exclusively. Because music had been such a powerful tool in my life for evil and had fed my depression, I had to make a solid decision regarding what kind of music I would allow into my mind and heart. I know this: all music is powerful.

It isn't just what we hear on the surface. There are messages (through the lyrics) attached to the music that give the songs the power to evoke emotion. Music is a gift or it can be a curse depending upon what its message is. Personally, I would rather listen to songs that glorify God so that I can grow in my faith. Life is hard enough without sabotaging myself with negative messages. Music that exalts Jesus also keeps the atmosphere around me positive and up lifting.

The lyrics in Christian music encourage me to keep walking in the right direction, to keep my eyes on Jesus, and to focus on the things of God. There's enough bad news in the world. I might as well fill my own space with good news, right? For me, Christian music is a powerful anti-depressant!

There's a lot of great Christian music out there, but if you don't know where to start, here are two artists that I would highly recommend: **Toby Mac** [12] (Christian Hip Hop. Especially his CD called, *"This is Not a Test"*) and **Big D & the Good News Blues**. [13] (Contact me at <u>dhaasbigd@gmail.com</u> if you want this music. I have personal connections.)

Could the Cause Of This Depression Be That I Have Set No Goals?

I guess I'm never as depressed as when I have no plans for the future. In any dictionary, the meaning of the word "hope" is to have expectation. Hope doesn't mean to "wish," though our society has certainly diminished the word. If we are filled with hope, then we are filled with expectation of something in the future.

People who are hope-less will contemplate suicide because they have no expectation of the future. That's why goals are vitally important in our battle with depression. As in football or soccer, the teams must get goals or touchdowns in order to win the game.

When we set and reach goals in our lives, they can help us achieve the bigger plan of a lifestyle of winning which translates into living with purpose. Reaching goals gives us great encouragement to carry on. But if we don't set any goals, if we have no plans, then we have nothing to shoot for. We will have no expectation for the future. We will be hope-less. At that point, we tend to give up.

If you are depressed, may I suggest you set some realistic goals for your day, your week, your month, in order to win the game? Goals and a plan just may be part of the lifeline you need to get out of the pit of depression.

Goals equal hope. Hope equals purpose. Purpose equals a reason to live.

Could The Cause Of This Depression Be That I Am An Artist?
(See Part 2, "There are women, there are men, and then there are ARTISTS.")

And Finally, Could the Cause of This Depression Be Spiritual?

The Spiritual Elephant in the Room—
The Mastermind Behind Suicide

It seems that in most circles where people talk about the prevention of suicide, they leave out the one invisible, yet crucial player in this deadly scenario, and that is, the devil. Chalk him up to imaginary religious foolishness if you want to, but that doesn't make him any less real or effective.

Jesus made it clear that the devil is our enemy. The devil's mission is mapped out for us in **John 10:10**. Jesus said, *"The thief comes only to steal and kill and destroy..."*

What did Jesus mean by "... steal, kill and destroy"? I don't think Jesus was talking about the devil actually having the authority to "kill" us (because he is a created angel and not God), but I do believe he can torment us to the point that we become so miserable that we might want to die.

The devil can't take our lives, so he **tries to steal** the quality of our lives. Through his lies and illusions, the devil **tries to kill** our hope for a future. If we don't have a vision for the future, if we don't have hope (expectation) then we will live a life of defeat and hopelessness. And finally, the devil wants to **destroy into a million pieces any semblance of a life of faith in God**.

The devil wants to lie to us and make us believe we're poor, but Jesus tells us the truth so that we can be rich in the things of God. Jesus said, *"I came that they may have life, and have it abundantly."* **(John 10:10)**

Tell me, who's stronger, God or the devil? Let me answer that, God is stronger and greater, and loves us more than we can fathom. I encourage you to call out to Him for help to determine what is causing your depression. He will answer you if you seek Him. He's done it for me. Why wouldn't He do it for you?

You Don't Know How I Feel

"You don't know how I feel." We've all heard this statement before. As a former depressed and suicidal person, I've said that exact statement and I've watched my relatives at a total loss as to how to help me.

Because I have experience on this end, I would like to talk to those of you who have depression now and those of you who are suicidal. I would like to speak to you in a straightforward way.

No, others don't know how we feel. How can they know how we feel? We don't communicate, we isolate, we push them away....I know, I know, it's all part of the dysfunction that happens inside of a person who is depressed.

How can we describe what we are feeling if we can't understand it ourselves?

That being said, I would like you to consider something. You may not have thought of this before or lately, but have you considered that you don't know how *they* feel on the other end? I think I can name how *they* feel in one word: "helpless."

These people who love you are trying desperately to help but always to no avail. When they do something extreme, like take you to a rehab program, oh, the things that you have said to them...

After a long time of not knowing how to help, eventually, even the best of them crumbles. They lose heart. You and I know how it feels to be helpless and hopeless. What did we do? Well, we got worn out and wanted to give up. However, their giving up doesn't look like our giving up. Their brokenness could look like anger or abandonment from our end.

They can't take the helpless feeling anymore. Maybe they're so tired of failing when it comes to helping you that for the sake of their own sanity, they leave, or stop listening.

One of the worst things we can do is to say, *"I'm going to take myself out of the equation so that they don't have to feel responsible for me anymore, so that they can get on with their lives without me holding them back. I will help my loved ones by killing myself. I'll leave them a note assuring them that my suicide was not their fault."*

Ok, let me say that is the worst possible idea in the world. Your death will most likely do the **exact opposite** of what you are trying to do. Instead of peace, your absence through suicide will cause chaos. Instead of letting them off the hook, your death will snag them forever. The note probably won't bring peace to them either.

One Mom that I interviewed had *memorized* the note from her son. **Memorized it**. From what I could discern, that note actually became an anchor that held her back from living her own life to the fullest.

May I make a more practical suggestion that could actually help to avoid such devastation? Tell those who are trying to help you that you appreciate their concern, but don't just tell them. Force yourself to let them help you by taking you out to lunch or coffee once in a while. Tell them how you're feeling instead of making them try to guess. Ask *them* to lunch. Let them in a little, and stop pushing them away. Thank them. Tell them when they've said something that's helped you. Send them a card every now and then.

I know that's next to impossible, but sometimes the way out of our own pit is to show appreciation and help someone else to know that while they may feel helpless, they are not useless, they are not failures. These family members and friends have feelings too. They aren't robots. And we aren't the only ones who feel bad. I know you know all this.

Sometimes the way we treat those who are trying to help us drives us deeper into depression because we know we're hurting them. I know, but if you always isolate, try doing something different next time, and call someone. Maybe they will need to talk to YOU that day! Maybe you could actually help *them*. Boy, I hope I'm not making you mad, but if it changes your future in a positive way, then I'll be glad to take the hit.

I'll do my best to put into words how "we" feel in the next part of the book that's written to those who truly may not understand this depression/suicidal issue. *"What we're dying to tell you."*

The Radiator, the Heater and the Exact Opposite of How You Feel

I don't know much about cars, but over the years I've learned something that could be useful in the battle against depression.

I've had a few junk cars in my day. More than once my car has overheated. If you can't stop and fix the problem, guess what you should do with a car that's overheating....are you ready? Turn the heat **ON** in the car.

That's right, the car is overheating and you should **turn on the heat** inside of the car. For those of us who are not mechanically inclined, or, like me, you don't understand the physics of why this solution works, it sounds like someone is pulling your leg. Turning on the heater in the car won't totally fix your problem, but it could help you get to a service station.

If we look at depression as if our engine is over-heating, then we need to do the exact thing we don't want to do in order to keep going down the road. Don't feel like calling someone when you are depressed? Call someone anyway. Don't want to go outside? Do the exact opposite of the way you *feel* and go outside. Don't feel like eating, or visiting, or going to the store? Eat, and go and do anyway.

Try doing the opposite of what you feel when you are depressed. It probably won't be the long term cure, but it may get you to a service station. It's just a thought.

Here are some quick suggestions to keep your car going forward in life:

Fifty Random Yet Really Useful Real-Life Recommendations That Could Perhaps Relieve the Rude Reality of Depression

*Read the Bible * make your bed * go to Church * create something * go out to eat with a friend * take your dog for a walk * turn on some Christian music * set a goal for today * go to a Bible Study * turn off the news and watch a feel-good movie * pray * draw or paint a picture of a cow in a field of green grass surrounded by yellow flowers * put together a puzzle * write a letter or send a card of encouragement to someone * buy yourself some flowers * visit someone in the hospital or nursing home * sing a song * call your Mom or someone who loves you like Mom * forgive everyone who has offended you * eat a steak * let go of all bitterness * pray for your enemies * call out to God * smile (even if you're alone) * confess your sins to another person *confess your sins to God * learn something new * praise God for who He is * read a good book * make some popcorn * go for a jog * eat a piece of fruit * have a cup of strong coffee * go to a Christian concert * take a bike ride * write in your journal * declare the promises of God * read the 23rd Psalm out loud * cook your best dish and invite someone to dinner * take a bubble bath *call someone * text a friend a compliment * thank God for at least 10 things in your life * sit outside and listen to the birds singing * buy a gift for someone for no particular reason * begin a project that you've been putting off * vacuum something * take a drive * play a board game with friends * kiss a baby * take a picture or * roast a marshmallow.

WHAT IF

You may be feeling like I'm simplifying your experience with depression, *"Certainly, it's not as easy as eating right, or getting a dog."* To which I say, that's probably true, but **WHAT IF** something on this list works to help you keep moving? What if you try some of these things and one, or a combination of them work? What if you tried something different or did the exact opposite of what you feel? What if you could feel better? Would you try something new?

My Story

As I said in the introduction to this book, I have my own personal story of attempted suicide. I guess that's one of the reasons I'm so passionate about helping those in this situation.

I remember myself drowning in a sea of despair during my younger years. If only I could have told my thirteen-year-old self what the future had in store for her, maybe she would have been able to *just hold on*.

Note to Self

Dear thirteen-year-old self,

I know you're going through some tough times right now. Your whole world has fallen apart through your dad's divorce from the only mom you really ever knew.

I realize this event has sent you reeling.

Now, you're in a brand new city in a brand new school and every day it's a brand new nightmare. The kids are making fun of you, and as a result you have crawled under a previously unfamiliar rock of insecurity.

You've made a decision. You will either become a star or you will kill yourself.

I know exactly how you feel. You feel lost, lonely, empty and alone. The music you listen to and sing with every day after the nightmare *which is school*, is most depressing, yet comforting at the same time.

As a child, you used to sing in public, but not anymore. Now you only sing to the radio in the room you share with Grandma in Florida.

I feel your pain grow as you allow these feelings of helplessness, betrayal, sadness, uselessness, and hopelessness to envelope you. Each and every day you are going deeper into the abyss.

No one really understands because you don't explain it to them. But really, "who would listen?" you reason.

You start to think about a way to stop this pain that has become a kind of faithful companion, and the only thing you can think to do is kill yourself.

I wish you could see yourself at forty-nine. I know, I know, in your mind, making it past even eighteen years old isn't supposed to happen.

But I'm here to tell you a story that will blow your mind. I know you're wearing a hat, so hold onto it 'cause I'm about to tell you exactly what your future holds.

In the next five years you will continue to deteriorate. You will struggle at school, oh, not because you don't have the brains to succeed, but because you're preoccupied with the idea of death.

You believe your future will be cut short, so why even try at school? You will self-medicate and try all kinds of drugs as a way to self-destruct.

While living in Florida, you will be put into a mental hospital where you will not get much help, but where you will learn how to commit suicide "the right way."

Even with your "new knowledge," you will search and search for the perfect way to **end** your life, but to no avail. And even this will be chalked up to yet another failure, because that's what the loudest voice inside has convinced you that **you are,** a failure.

You will have these certain phrases that are on a continuous loop in your mind: *"Do everyone a favor and kill yourself," "You've gone so far even God has given up on you.*" Oh, and this is one of the worst things you will hear in your head: *"You're so worthless, even your own mother abandoned you."*

But there's this other voice inside that says, *"What about Grandma? My suicide will ruin her life."* Every day for five years, you will contemplate suicide, and even attempt it several times in a flirting kind of way. It's a miserable way to live, but you will be convinced that suicide is the only way out.

Not long after your eighteenth birthday, you will drive to Ohio to meet your birth mother whom you haven't seen since you were three years old.

Alcohol had destroyed her family and her life, but these many years later, she will have become a Christian. For some reason you won't like that idea. True to form, during your first night at her house, you will cut your wrist. The next morning when she finds out what you have done, she will say something that you will remember for the rest of your life.

Instead of putting you into a program or calling the cops, she will speak these words to you, "I'm not going to send you anywhere. I'm going to trust my God with you." Although you will be over-joyed with her response, your pleasure will be short-lived as you get mad at her for something trivial and take off for Florida once again.

Months will pass and the voices will become so loud that you can hardly stand it, "GIVE UP!"

In February of 1986, you will do just that. You will no longer care about anyone whom you may hurt by your suicide. You will no longer factor in your previous fear of spending an eternity in Hell. You will be totally under the control of the devil himself.

At this point, you will make your first serious attempt at suicide by slitting your wrist. The last thing you will remember is the blood squirting into the air as your body crumples into a pile on the bathroom floor.

You will wake the next morning with a tube sock wrapped around your wrist, courtesy of the forty year old man that you are living with. You won't care that you were unsuccessful. You will try it again that night. And again the next night.

The night after that, you will have a vivid dream of a man telling you that you have **"one week to live."** You will interpret it that God will never come to save your soul again. You may live on the earth, but whenever you do die, you will spend eternity in Hell.

This shakes you out of your slumber, but only to the degree that you get drunk for three days out of the seven that you think you have left. This doesn't sound like a very good life, I know, but hold on, you're about to meet someone Who will literally SAVE your life and GIVE you a future filled with hope!

On the fourth day after the dream, before you go to bed, you will pray this prayer, and it will change your life forever: "**God, if You're real, I need You to show me.**"

I'm here to tell you that from that exact moment on, you will be gloriously saved. That very day you will meet Jesus, your Creator. You will wake up the next morning and be a brand new person from the inside out!

Where you were once empty, you will be filled to overflowing with HOPE and LIFE and a confidence that you haven't had a whiff of since you were a small child. From that day on, you will never again need drugs or alcohol because Jesus will be all you need.

Ah, the music. What happens with the music and your singing? Well, a few months after you get saved, you will start attending a big church. It's there that you pick up your public singing again.

You never will hit stardom *per se*, but you will get to do something even cooler than that: throughout your life, you will get tons of opportunities to sing for God! You will record one tape, two professional Blues CDs and several other CDS all filled with original music.

That's right. The Lord will allow you to create songs out of nothing. Not only will you sing songs, but you will write songs, too! But wait, I have to tell you something else that's very important.

I know you never want to get married because you think no one stays together anyway, but guess what? You will say, *"I do!"* You will marry a guy who loves you and who will help you to fulfill a spiritual calling that God will give to you.

This guy (his name is Curt) is a big reason that you will do concerts and make those tapes and CDs I mentioned earlier. He will just happen to be a sound man and a recording engineer, and a super smart guy who will bring you joy on many levels.

Will your marriage stay together? You betcha! I'll tell you more about that later.

On a different note, you know how you're suffering right now and being made fun of because of your hair? Well, it turns out that your sister-in-law, Kelley, will be a HAIR DRESSER! Thanks to her, your hair, which has been the bane of your existence, will turn out to be one of your best assets. It's crazy, but at one point, your hair will become an actual style that people will pay good money for! No kidding.

I know this is hard to believe, but I still have more to tell you.

After spending your whole adolescence alone with virtually no real friends, guess what? Jesus will give you deep friendships with other Christians. Through these relationships, God will heal you, teach you, and help you grow up. Some of these people will be friends for a time in your life, and many of them will become lifetime friends.

You see, what you think is impossible right now (having real friends and being happy) will become a reality for you if you *just hold on.*

And just when you think your life couldn't get any more bizarre, not only will you get married, but you will have two sons! Sorry, I should have told you to sit down first before blurting that out.

You'll name them Levi and Jonathan after guys in the Bible. They will grow up to be fine, young men who will make you proud and bring joy to your soul. But it gets even better than that. They will each get married to talented women who love Jesus, and you will love them too! Can you even imagine this?

You will become a wife, a mother and a mother-in-law! Are you sitting down yet? Because I'm about to send your mind into orbit. When you are forty-eight years old, your oldest son, Levi and his wife, will have a child. I bet you never thought that YOU would be a Grandma, but you will be!

Are you catching what I'm throwing here?

You never actually win a Grammy for music, but you will become a Grammy! How cool is that? And all of this is fine and dandy, but I bet you're wondering if you will finally be happy in the future.

That's a good question and I'm so glad you asked. The answer to that question is a resounding, YES! But "happy" isn't really the right word. It's more like content, filled, satisfied and over-the-top blessed.

But yeah, I guess happy works too.

By the way, you will move to the Upper Peninsula of Michigan in 2010 and will absolutely LOVE it! You will live in a really small town, which is weird, after growing up in the suburbs.

Truth be told, you won't want to move there from Florida at first, but the strange thing is, that in *that* place you will find *your* place. God planted some really cool seeds in you a long time ago that will come to fruition in the years you spend living in the U.P.

It's a good feeling to be doing *what* you know God wants you to do *where* He wants you to be doing it. Among many other things, you will lead worship music at a great Church (you will learn how to play guitar shortly after you become a Christian), you'll help teach Bible Studies, and write a column in a newspaper.

There's more. Hold onto your seat. Right now, this very day, in 2016 you will be writing your first book.

WRITING A BOOK!

It's a book about suicide called, *"just hold on."* God is going to use your experience with suicide and sadness to help others!

Would you look at that, you don't actually turn out to be a loser after all.

So you see, you have a future. As dark as it is for you at thirteen, it will get darker. But if you *just hold on*, you will not only survive, you will love life, AND through your relationship with Jesus, you will be a help to others who are hurting.

At present, you are celebrating twenty eight years of marriage, and thirty years as a Christian. You've seen the Lord deliver on every one of His promises to you without fail.

It's funny. Your default is to give up when things get tough, but after you meet Jesus, when everything comes against you, you just want to try harder. You don't see any sign of quitting.

Your future is secure and you plan to serve Jesus with your very last breath.

Note to self: Just hold on. God has great things in store for you. Your future is real and it's beautiful. It's not always easy, but today, you have no regrets, you try your best, and countless people are blessed as a result. In fact, some people will actually exist because you didn't give up. Because when you think about it, it's not just *your* future you're deciding today.

Just hold on, life will get better. I promise.

Real LIFE Success Stories

"She tried and failed at death, but held on and succeeded at life" dh

*From The Interviews

Here's how life turned out for two people who failed at
the attempt at suicide, but held on and succeeded in life.

Christina

Struggling with childhood memories of physical
abuse and an aftermath of feeling worthless and alone,
Christina made her first unsuccessful suicide attempt at
the age of fifteen. Lacking purpose for living, in her late
teens, she turned to alcohol and drugs. Her downward
spiral continued and eventually led to two more suicide
attempts.

In her mid-twenties, Christina had a career and many
material possessions, but was completely empty inside.
She was writing songs for a hobby and learning to play
guitar when one day, Christina heard the voice of God say
to her, *"When are you going to start writing songs for
Me?"* That was the day everything changed for Christina.
That was the day she says, *"I was filled with purpose."*

Today, she is a wife and mother of two and a grandma.
Among other things, she is the author of three books, a

songwriter, musician, media producer, and minister of Jesus Christ.

Christina's main goal every day is to help someone find hope. She uses social media as an avenue to spread a message of encouragement through her blog: www.new-strength.wordpress.com. Millions of people have been blessed by her Praise in Motion Music YouTube channel for kids at: www.youtube.com/ PraiseInMotionMusic, and many have found hope on her website: christina-cooklee.com.

If Christina had succeeded in death, she would not have been able to help countless people to thrive and to love life. Ironically, Christina was told as a child that she "would not amount to much," **but look at her now!** Because she held on, Christina's life is LIVING proof that God can turn our messes into messages and make beauty out of ashes.

Don't give up. Even though you can't see it right now, you have a beautiful future full of purpose and life. It's just up ahead of you, but you've got to *hold on*.

Brian

After 27 years in prison, being addicted to drugs, run-ins with the law, satanism, and a hate-filled, violent life, Brian has become a faithful husband, father of four and a minister of the Gospel of Jesus Christ. Through his motorcycle ministry and other avenues, he is a speaker and encouragement to people all over the country.

When asked the question: "How is this world better because you are still in it?" His answer was, *"I'm one more warrior for the Kingdom. One more voice letting people know there's hope in this dying world."*

Some of Brian's tattoos will tell you that his past was steeped in darkness, but his life today tells a different story of light and life. Brian's life proves that no one is too far gone for God to save them, and to use them for the good of the world and to the glory of God. So, *just hold on*, your future is brighter than you can imagine.

*From the Interviews -*A note from those who had attempted suicide.*
My questions: "What finally helped? How do you cope? And in what ways are you glad that you did not succeed in taking your own life?"

Lauren: "I grew up. I just woke up and said, 'I'm tired of living this way.' I got rid of all of the negative influences. Today, I love my life, my friends and family. I'm glad I didn't succeed."

Christina: *"What finally helped me was Jesus, and some Christian counseling. The main thing was hearing from God Who gave me a purpose for living. I continue to* cope by doing what God called me to do, following Jesus and helping others to find hope and encouragement."

Brian: "I became a Christian and I grew up. My Mom also helped me a lot. Today, I cope by following Jesus and helping others to find their way to Him."

Julia: "Counseling, growing up and holding on is what finally helped me. I cope today by sleeping, crocheting, walking the dog, keeping busy, and cleaning."

Mary: "Counseling helped me. I'm so glad that I didn't succeed because I can't imagine what my death by suicide would have done to my children. They would have never recovered. I cope today by helping others."

Part Two

To Those Who Grieve the Loss of a Loved One to Suicide

T ruth be told, grieving was the subject that motivated the idea for this book. Because of my own attempts at suicide, I had been asked to speak at a suicide prevention event. At that event I saw one of the saddest things I had ever seen.

One of the speakers was the father of a daughter who had taken her own life. The man was so distraught that every word he spoke was like he was reliving the tragedy all over again. I thought, "Lord, please help this man. Surely, he just lost his daughter." I was floored when I found out that his daughter's suicide occurred a full six years earlier.

It prompted the question in me, *"Is the grief caused by suicide different from the grief caused by other ways of dying?"* I wanted to find out the difference in grief if there was any, but I also wanted to find out how those folks had coped in order to help others grieve. I wondered how those of us who have never lost a person to suicide could help *them*. I wanted to know what to say to them.

I then created a series of questions as it related to their loss, and set out to interview those who have suicide grief. What I found was that grief is grief, no matter how the death happens. Death will bring loss, no matter how it occurred.

However, there seems to be at least one common element in the hearts and minds of those who lose loved ones to suicide, and that is guilt. The questions, the regrets, the mistakes, the loss all equal a suffering that can bring a despair all its own. Hard grief. Long grief. Survivor's grief.

Coping for those left behind
Rest from Your Battle with Regret

"Having a dialogue with regret is like accepting an invitation to dance with the devil." dh

Regret: a feeling of sadness, or disappointment over something that has happened.

Regret is a natural response to making a mistake, but if left unresolved, it can become a monster. Regret can take over and become an unhealthy filter through which we run all of our future experiences. *It taints our future by placing blame on the past.* It creates undeserved guilt, and reminds us that we made a mistake that can never be remedied. Regret makes a terrible roommate, and personally, I've decided to kick it out of my house.

Just the other day, I made a mistake. *I zigged when I should have zagged.* It wasn't a sin, though it was a mistake that I could not undo. Although no one was hurt in that scenario, I believe I made the wrong choice. I could dwell on my mistake and be miserable, or I could forget it and go on (forget regret!).

The next thing I knew, I was saying this out loud, *"I don't regret it, but I won't repeat it."* See what happened there? I acknowledged my mistake without regret taking any power to ruin my day, or worse, my future. I will do it right the next time because I'm not dwelling on my past mistake. This is what you could call "maintaining mental health."

***"Time doesn't heal all wounds, but God can heal all wounds in time"* dh**

The Remedy for Regret

Regret for a mistake is one thing, but when it comes to losing someone to suicide, there can be no end to the

83

havoc regret can cause if we're not careful. Still, how we deal with small regret or big regret starts, I think, with taking only the responsibility that is ours to take.

I believe one of the most tragic scars that suicide leaves on those left behind are the questions. *"Was there something I could have done to stop this person from dying?"* *"Maybe if I would have been more loving, or not so busy, or if I had only answered the phone that day, would he still be alive?"*

I imagine the questions can become paralyzing in themselves if we don't find some kind of resolution. Between the guilt and the regret there has to be hope in there somewhere. In fact, I think I have a sliver of peace and freedom to offer you.

It Was NOT YOUR FAULT

In some of my interviews, I was able to share a freeing truth with some of those who are still shackled by the question: was it my fault? I'm here to tell you that according to what I see in Scripture, it absolutely **WAS NOT** your fault.

Some will believe what I'm about to say, and some will not, but I hope all will at least consider what I'm trying to convey.

For me, it all started with my Grandma who died a few years ago. When it happened, I was convinced that she was killed by the medical system. For months I was angry, until one day, when I was memorizing **Psalm 139,** I came to verse **16**: *"Your eyes have seen my unformed substance; and in Your book were all written the days that were ordained for me, when as yet there was not one of them."*

I thought about that, *"the days that were ordained for me...."* Then I reasoned that there are a certain "number of days" that are given to each one of us.

We don't die from cancer or accidents, or even suicide. We die when the number of our days are up. Our time simply runs out. No one dies too soon or too late. If the death wasn't by suicide then it would have been by some other way on that particular day. I guess that means that we are kind of indestructible until our days are done here on earth. Still, *I don't understand the way, but I understand that there is a day.*

A specific **Life-Time** is given to each human being by the Creator of all things. No matter how, we will all die on the day we were ordained to die. That's what I see in the Scriptures, and that truth set me free from blaming people for the death of my Grandma. In fact, I don't blame anyone for someone dying anymore.

Don't get me wrong, I hate death, but it's no one's fault. If you choose to believe that God is in charge of both the day of birth and the day of death, you can be set free right now from any kind of survivor's guilt. Yes, you and I have made mistakes even with our loved ones, but the best thing we can do with those mistakes is to learn from them and try to help others to find peace in the midst of their own nightmare of suicide.

The way I see it, even our mistakes are NOT the cause of anyone's death. It's not your fault that your loved one died. You are not responsible for the life or death of another human being. Only God can control that. We just have to do the best we can to live out the number of days God has given to each one of us in a way that pleases Him.

Grieving the Answers

Those of us who have not experienced grief from suicide will never fully understand your pain, but at least we can acknowledge that it exists. At least we can try to help you in your recovery and pray for your healing.

Did you know that you are a precious creation of God, too? Did you know that God sees your suffering and that He's never left you alone? All of us can find our comfort in Him. Only God can understand and fix your broken heart. And He wants to do just that.

One day as I was grieving the loss of my friend who had died, I asked the Lord, *"Why am I grieving so hard for her?"*

There had been some conflict in our friendship that had caused some questions in me. I had wanted to ask her about these things, but every time I would try, I realized that it wouldn't be good for her health. She was sick, and I didn't want to upset her.

Even on her deathbed, I couldn't ask her about these things that troubled me because obviously, it wasn't about me. She was dying and it was my job to be there for her. About four months after she died, I received the answer to my question.

I believe God showed me that I wasn't necessarily grieving the loss of my friend, as much as I was grieving the *loss of the answers to the questions* that I had for her. She took the answers with her to the grave, and now I would never know this side of Heaven.

It was at this point that I had a profound encounter with the Lord. I verbally needed to release the answers I was grieving to God. As I did that, I felt an immediate peace wash over me. But then I sensed something else that the Lord was giving to me. He reminded me that He is the God of all answers, and that nothing is impossible for Him. He knew the answers to the questions I had for my friend and if He saw fit, He could tell me.

I didn't have to grieve the answers. They were still there. It didn't take too long before I just didn't need to know anymore. The hard grief I was feeling lifted from that day on. I have no more regrets, and the need for answers no longer consumes me. God can do anything, and we can ask Him for anything (**John 14:14**).

If you have questions about your loved one, why not take them to the only One Who knows the answer?

*From the Interviews

Every person grieves differently, but I wanted to find out what helped those who were grieving the suicide death of their loved one. I wanted to know what things were helpful during their grieving process and what things were not helpful.

This is what I found:

Helpful Grief Responses: people were sympathetic, prayed, brought meals, sent texts, came for short visits, sent cards, offered to talk about deceased loved one, gave hugs, said, *"I'm sorry for your loss."* From a Mom: *"One of the most helpful cards I got said, 'I don't know what to say. I love you.'"*

Not Helpful Grief Responses: awkward, tried to ignore the situation, wouldn't talk about loved one, too much attention, tried to give advice.

One More Thought For Those Who Grieve

The 23rd Psalm is a wonderful and comforting portion of Scripture that continues to help people through the process of grieving. You may have heard this verse at your loved one's memorial service. *"Even though I walk through the valley of the shadow of death, I will fear no evil for Thou art with me; Thy rod and Thy staff, they comfort me."* (Psalm 23:4)

As I was thinking about this verse the other day, I was struck with this part of it, *"Even though I WALK THROUGH the valley of the shadow of death...."*

Notice that we "walk through" the valley. We don't stop. We walk through. We may walk slowly, but we cannot ever stop in that valley of the shadow of death. We aren't meant to stop there. Whether it's our time of death or we're grieving the death of another, none of us is meant to stay in the valley of the shadow of death.

I think because of regret and other things, many people have not only stopped in that valley after the tragedy of suicide, but they have built homes there. The darkness of the shadow has become so normal to them that they feel more comfortable in their sorrow of death than in the light of the living.

If you have built a house there in that valley, I implore you, get up and move! God doesn't want you to live in the shadow of death any longer. He never meant for you to put down roots in that valley, but only to **walk through** that darkness.

Do you know what causes a shadow? Light is the reason for the shadow. An object (death in this case) displaces the light for a time causing a shadow of darkness to form. If we keep moving toward the light, that shadow will disappear from our presence. Not because it moved away from us, but because we moved away from it.

What do you think the last part of that verse means: *"...Thy rod and Thy staff, they comfort me...."*?

Simplistically speaking, the rod of the shepherd was used to discipline the sheep and also as a defensive tool to protect the sheep. The staff, with its curved top was more for gently guiding the sheep or for lifting them out of precarious situations.

So, how do the rod and staff comfort us when we walk through the valley of the shadow of death and darkness? Because God is holding the rod, we know that nothing will hurt us, and He is using the staff to keep us moving toward the light and out of the valley.

Yes, we will grieve. It's part of being human, but we can't put down roots in death. We can't effectively live there or we will not survive. *Death is a part of life, but death doesn't have to be our life.*

Part Three

To Those Who Would Like More Insight Into the "Subject" of Suicide

A Glimpse Into the Mind of a Person With Suicidal Tendencies

It occurred to me in this writing process that a lot of folks don't have any idea what goes on in the minds of those who are suicidal. As a former suicidal person, I have the unique perspective of what it feels like to want to commit suicide.

Knowing how hard it must be for those who have not experienced these mental and emotional challenges, in this next section, I will attempt to put into words some of the struggles of those who contemplate suicide.

The Dance With Suicide

Suicide starts with a fleeting thought. Depending on what's going on in your life, and even if nothing terrible is happening to you, for some reason you decide to entertain this thought of suicide...get to know it a little better, spend more time with the idea. Then It asks you to dance, but it lets you lead... at first, and for a while.

Before you know it, and if no one 'cuts in' (that is, none of your friends or family notices the signs of despair, and Who it is that you're dancing with), Suicide starts to lead the dance.
This dance that started as a waltz has become a familiar, and strangely comfortable embrace, a slow dance; but almost without warning, the embrace mutates into some kind of evil, monstrous death grip that you have no power nor the desire to be loosed from. There is still hope to escape this hold that Death has on a person. As long as we are still breathing, there is hope. (dh)

Is Suicide a Selfish Act?

I don't believe that suicide is a purely selfish act. For me, suicide was far from selfish.

I spent five hard years trying to figure out the perfect suicide. One that showed my pain, but that didn't cause others to feel like it was their fault. For all my trying and wasted time, *thankfully,* I never did find the perfect suicide.

Others have felt that their suicide would actually *help* their loved ones. They mistakenly thought they were a burden and if they were out of the picture then their family and friends could be happy. That's not selfishness, that's deception.

Others find themselves in such a jam with the law, a broken relationship, or secret sin that they just can't see any way out of the situation or that it could ever be remedied. Having no hope for the future does not equal selfishness, it seems to me that it adds up to pure desperation. By the time I got to the point of a serious attempt, I had lost all concept of others or life or anything that used to matter.

What's worse than an abundance of feelings? Having no feelings at all. It was like I was a robot. At the end, I just kind of did what I was told. No person was leading me to do it. I was not in control.

There's a real power at work that can take *broken human beings* and convince them to throw THEMSELVES off of the proverbial cliff. But if you dance with something-anything long enough, it will take *you* over. It's much like addiction in that there is a point where we lose control of our lives. It's desperation we feel right before it gets to that point though. It's like there is no other option.

That's one of the main reasons I wrote this book. I want people to see that there are alternatives to the worst case scenario of suicide. If we can get folks to look at these things before they can't see straight, then I believe some will see the logic of holding on and begin to accept the help that's being offered. Ultimately, I don't think suicide is about selfishness, I think it's about an addiction to sadness that people wrongly think cannot be satisfied with anything but death.

It's about stopping the pain (which is real), and in the process (they think) they are trying to lift the burden of themselves off of others.

In reality, we know that their attempts to relieve those who love them are actually causing lifetime burdens to be put on those people they are trying to protect. It's about permanently punishing ourselves for something we don't realize that God will forgive us for. It's about feeling like we've gone too far and there is no hope for us. Lies, yes. Selfishness? I don't think so.

Suicide is a complicated issue and people have different reasons for wanting to do it.

One very interesting thing I have seen from my research is that many of those who are suicidal are also creative, deep thinking individuals. I've come to call them *Artists*. This next section will give brand new insight into some of the personalities of those who are most likely to contemplate suicide.

There Are Women, There Are Men, and Then There Are ARTISTS

You may not know it by looking at me, but if you've ever had a conversation with me, then you can pick this up: I am deep. My mind virtually never stops philosophizing, thinking, getting ideas.

Mostly, I get word ideas, not so much practical, inventive things, more like ideas relating to the human condition. I also, write, sing and play guitar. I am an Artist. It took me a long time to admit that, actually. Yes, I am a woman, but from what I'm gathering, being an artist supersedes gender.

I started to think that there are three kinds of people: men, women, and **Artists.**

You might be an Artist if ....

Artists don't usually "fit in" to society's mold. They are often times convinced that there is something wrong with them. Many times an Artist's love language is "words of affirmation," so please be careful what you say to us. Your words can build us up to the stars or they can grind us down to the deepest hole in the ground— a hole that we may have a really hard time climbing out of.

Yes, we are intense. Yes, we are deep thinkers. Yes, we may talk too much, or not at all. Yes, we can tend to isolate. Yes, we can be super-duper sensitive. Yes, we are consistently inconsistent, and may have trouble finishing things, or not. And yes, sometimes we need people to help us not to implode or self destruct, but that doesn't mean the world doesn't need Artists. And no, we are not lazy. When we have a project, we will pour our whole selves into it.

What if Artists are the reason we have inventions, innovation, and progress? Even the scientific community, as they are allowed to think outside of the box, is largely (I'm convinced) made up of Artists.

That being said, please don't offer us a pill, or a "**suck it up cupcake**" solution to our Artist-ness. Just because we're deep, doesn't mean we're weak. In fact, Artists may just be some of the most courageous people on the planet. Why, you ask? Well, in spite of our insecurities and fears (and there are many), we go right ahead and risk everything when we perform or even show our work to another human being. It takes a lot of guts to stand in front of one person or many people and "share" your gift. And isn't courage just doing something even if you are afraid?

To My Artist Sisters

Artists are just plain different. If you happen to be a female Artist, then you have at least one "special" obstacle to overcome, such as P.M.S. which can hit you like a freight train EVERY MONTH for 40 years! Artists are already intense, but add hormones to the mix, and you have potential for a volcanic eruption the magnitude of Mount Vesuvius!

But wait, there's more. If you are a CHRISTIAN FEMALE ARTIST, I don't know what to tell you. Now you have spiritual warfare, hormones, and the weirdness of an Artist all rolled into one. I honestly don't know how I've made it this far without going crazy. (dh)

A Very, Very Interesting Revelation

In my continuing unscientific research, it was confirmed (to me at least) that most people who contemplate and or attempt suicide seem to be deep thinkers with a very creative personality. **They are artists, musicians, painters, writers, poets, actors, dancers, inventors...**

When I did a Google search for people who had committed suicide, I found that the vast majority of the hundreds of people who took their own lives fell into one of the above listed creative categories. This fact is further proven when you read or watch almost any biography of a famous musician, actor, painter, or writer. In their stories, you will find a group of seriously complicated people whose lives were ruined by addiction, whose lives were characterized by struggle with their craft, and whose lives were ultimately destroyed by the inability to control it.

In cases of famous people, I'm thinking that it was the fame that kicked their personality challenges into high gear. They just couldn't navigate the rough seas of fame, so they eventually gave up trying to steer their own ship.

Because creative people are often sensitive and deep, they need to be equipped with the necessary coping skills to control their thoughts. If they don't get a handle on *who* they are and *how* they are, they will inevitably go too far and too deep, ending up in a pit they cannot actually escape from on their own.

"PLEASE LISTEN TO ME!"
What we're dying to tell you

*From the Interviews
Here are some answers from those I interviewed in response to the question: *"Name something someone could have said to change your mind about attempting suicide."*

"You are not a burden. You matter." Lauren

"Any words from my Mom." Brian

"Absolutely nothing." Julia

"If someone would have shown me that I had a purpose in this world. If I had felt valued." Christina

We Don't Need a Pill, We Need a Project and a Purpose!

Since these people are gifted, I have found that the treatment for a depressed, Artist-type person may be that they need to be actively involved in what they are gifted to do.

It's unfortunate that when budget cuts come into the schools, the usual victims are music, art, and other things the government considers "non-essential" or "elective." I can tell you from my experience that there is nothing "non-essential" about singing, or writing, for me. These gifts, talents and artistic bents are not electives for people who are creative. **They are actually necessary for our sanity.**

Part Four

To Those in the Schools (Students & Educators)

New screening criteria for students?

In light of the revelation about "Artists," when it comes to mental health screening criteria in the schools, what if, instead of screening for depression, we start checking specifically for creativity?

Because when you think about it, isn't everyone depressed at one point in his or her life? Especially teenagers. Wow, I don't know if anyone has it easy in middle school and high school. And because of that, I think screening for depression is too large of a net.

What if we make the net smaller, and look for those people who are deep thinkers and loners, as those who are most at risk of suicide? AND when we find out who they are, instead of giving them a lifetime mental diagnosis with a medication to go with it, why don't we give them a project instead? Why don't we give them the customized tools to cope with their unique creative personalities?

As I think about my own experience, if I could have been involved in some kind of choir or even drama class (the writing and singing parts) in school, I just might have been able to pull out of the tailspin I was in. As it was, I battled with suicidal thoughts throughout my entire adolescence.

Today, I'm most happy when I'm doing what I'm gifted to do. Creative people need to find what they're good at and be encouraged and equipped to work out their anxiety and energy within their talent context. As we sing, dance, act, write, paint, draw, etc. we are fulfilled, we have something to pour ourselves into. As we function in those projects, we can find at least a portion of our purpose for being on this earth, and that's extremely helpful to us.

Like I said before, insecurity can be rampant in creative people. One of the best ways to combat that enemy is to **be active in our craft.** As we do what we're gifted to do, we feel confident that we matter, that we can be useful, and that we have purpose for being. As we share our work, people are blessed, and I think this is one of the greatest joys of an Artist. To encourage others is extremely satisfying and leads to our good mental health.

Suicide is the second leading cause of death in 15-24 year olds [6]

I wrote the following piece a few years ago after learning of a student who had taken his life.

Suicide in School-A Christian Response
My Mission as a Christian

God forbid this should ever happen in your school, but if it does, here is your mission as a Christian in light of this present darkness.

"You didn't see it coming and you couldn't stop it. Like so many others, you felt a pit in your stomach when you heard the news that your friend took his own life. It wasn't just when you heard the initial news though. Every time you think of your friend it's a new level of devastation that almost engulfs your entire mind for a minute.

There are no words that anyone can say to you right now. Nevertheless, you have a job to do. You have a mission from God right now that, strangely enough, was created by this tragedy. You are called to be strong in your faith, you are called to lead others to hope.

It's not your job to fix everyone or be God to them, but it is your calling to rise up in your faith and bring Jesus into their midst. It may be that you give counsel, but we should also not underestimate the power of just being there to listen to the broken hearts of others.

That said, you must not try to muster this strength from within yourself. Before you step foot on the campus, or answer a phone call, or respond through social media, please go to Jesus. People need to hear the voice of their Creator right now.

For such a time as this, you have been saved and placed in this unfathomable moment of darkness. Like Daniel in the Old Testament (please read Daniel, chapter one), you are a teenager. Also like Daniel, you have been sucked into a situation that is extremely desperate. What you do now can powerfully and positively affect a great many of your peers who are drowning in a sea of guilt and hopelessness because of this event.

Rise up, Christian! If you've been lax in your relationship with God, it's time to get real and get right with Him. Be bold, preach the Gospel, pray for your friends, encourage your friends at school, and everywhere you see them. Begin to make a practice of sending cards, texts, emails, and Facebook messages.

We are lights in this world, **(Matthew 5:14)** and the very source of that light dwells within us (Jesus). You are a mighty warrior called up to the front lines to be a weapon of righteousness **(Romans 6:13)** in the very hands of God Almighty. You are now fighting, not for the one who has been lost, but for those who have been left behind.

But before you do anything for others, I again implore you to seek your God, alone in prayer, for as long as it takes to find Him in a real and personal way. Make sure you really know Him through His Son, Jesus Christ. Seek Him and ask Him to search your heart, to heal your heart, then to empower you to be *HIS mouthpiece* to this dying world.

As a true Christian, and through the power and presence of Jesus Christ, you have been commissioned to GO. And remember, you are not alone. God is with you, as well as your older sisters and brothers in Christ. We are right behind you, cheering you on both in prayer, in counsel (if needed), and in word.

Don't question if you are qualified. As a Christian it is *'God who is at work in you, both to will and to do of HIS good pleasure.'* (**Philippians 2:13**) Not only that, but through the indwelling of the Holy Spirit, the Word of God, and prayer, you are more than equipped for any task the LORD may call you to. You are more than a conqueror in Jesus' name (**Romans 8:37**) and in Jesus' power.

Now, go forth in faith and be amazed at how our mighty God will use you to strengthen the weary for His renown and glory.

My fellow Christians, shine the light of Christ in this present darkness... it's our only mission in this life." dh

A Personal Note to Bullies

*Dear Bully: Believe it or not, you are one of the reasons that I have written this book. I want to give a voice to your victims, and I also want to open your eyes to see how **your life** could be so much better.*

I know you are insecure and you try to hide your inadequacies and fear under a mask of confidence and cruelty. You're probably not comfortable in your own skin. Only you know just how frightened and weak you really are on the inside. But you haven't always been like this. Somewhere along the line, in your short time on this earth, you were not valued. I want to ask who did this to you?

*Is it because when you go home at night, **you yourself** are being bullied and abused by a sibling, parent, a neighbor, or other relative? Are you lashing out at others because it brings some relief to your own wounded heart? Perhaps school is the only place where you feel that you have any control. So you get your satisfaction at the expense of another human being. Regardless of your reasons, your actions are unacceptable, and they must stop.*

Maybe you honestly don't understand what kind of torment your bullying is imposing upon others. Allow me to give you a first-hand look at the damage you are inflicting. You are dismantling a perfectly fine creation of God and rebuilding a monster in your own distorted image. Stripping them of their confidence and self-worth, you are planting seeds of a lifetime of self hate, and you are helping set a person on a course for self destruction.

I know because that's what the bullies did to me.

*Do you think God will look kindly on you, or over-look your childish, and seemingly harmless behavior? Do you think this stuff is not hurting you, too? Have you ever heard this saying, **"Do not be deceived, God is not mocked; for whatever a man sows, this he will also reap."**? In other words, if you sow (plant) **seeds** of evil (bullying, racism, etc.) you will reap a **harvest** of hate.*

Do you realize that God is not on your side in this? This may be news to you, but the God of the universe is actually opposed to what you are doing, and HE is on the side of your victim. I love that about God. He's always for the underdog, the unpopular one, and for those who are despised. **(1 Corinthians 1:27-28)**

Every single human being is equally valued by God, including you. As mean as you are right now, God still loves you and wants to save you. When Jesus is really our Lord, we no longer want to hurt people. In fact, as Christians, we become new creations. Everything about us becomes new, and we find joy in helping and giving courage to people. This kind of attitude is beneficial to society, but what you are doing is the stuff of confusion, rebellion, death, and revenge.

At the end of the proverbial day, you will have to answer for your actions in this regard. Stop fighting against God. Stop trying to prove your self-worth by tearing down another person, and stop pretending that you are better than someone else by making them feel like garbage.

Dear bully, don't continue to wreck the lives of others. Focus on the work that needs to be done in you. There's a confident joy in accepting people for who they are, what they look like, and even how they act. It's a peaceful feeling not to walk in arrogance and self-righteousness.

Please consider what you are doing, call on Jesus, and let Him turn you around 180 degrees. Your life could be so much better.

Instead of pushing someone over the edge, why not help them to *just hold on*.

Sincerely,

Denise, aka Big D

A former victim of bullying

A Word to the Bullied

You just hold on and pray. Your help is on the way. In the meantime, don't let bitterness overtake you. In Romans 12:21, we find this powerful and applicable truth, *"Do not be overcome by evil, but overcome evil with good."* God is with you to help you, but you need to call out to Him. He will give you the strength to pray for your enemy, and things will start to change, I can assure you of that. Prayer is a powerful weapon in our fight against discouragement. We are never helpless as long as we can pray. I wish I had known this when I was being made fun of in the seventh grade. It's empowering to think that we can connect to the ultimate Champion, and because of Him we will never have to be victims again. *Just hold on.*

A Warning to the Bystanders

Stop standing by and allowing someone to be bullied right in front of you or on social media. Stand up, speak up, and step up to their defense. Make no mistake, your silence in the face of abuse is wrong, too. Remember the holocaust. Many people never stepped in to stop the Nazis (bullies) because they were afraid for their own lives, but as long as the enemy was not *their* enemy, they were fine. One day though, their enemy came for *them*, but then it was too late to stand up, and there was no one left to stand up for them. So, find some courage and stand up to the bullies that are around you. God will reward you when you help the helpless.

Part Five

To Those Who Want Help and Who Want to Help

This Culture of Death

We live in a culture of death. Whether it's murder (including abortion), euthanasia, or suicide, death is a prevailing theme in our world. When it comes to suicide though, it's not just the youth who are taking their own lives.

I was shocked to discover that the elderly are also a high-risk group for suicide. *One in every four suicide attempts by the elderly ends in death.* [7] Why is this happening? I think it has a lot to do with the devaluation of life in general, but with the elderly, I'm sure it's even more personal. As they age, they lose almost everything that is dear to them. From spouses, to friends, to family, career, physical ability, to their homes, their pets, their possessions and finally, the elderly have lost society's respect for them.

Devaluing the Elderly

I've noticed that in America we no longer see the elderly as useful and beneficial to society. Older people are largely "thrown away."

The very basic need of every human being is to be needed— to matter to someone. Because we don't talk to them anymore, or they can't tell us, we don't realize that the lady in room 320 used to be the *Director of Nursing* of the very nursing home where she is now a resident. Or that the guy down the hall who can no longer speak and must be fed his meals used to be the *CEO* of a large company.

In the halls of nursing homes all over this country, there are musicians and scientists, writers and evangelists, professors, doctors, and ship's captains. They are Moms and Dads, and the Grandparents of a hundred grandchildren.

At one time in their lives, they were invaluable to their families. They have fought in wars for us, lost family and limbs in battle, and they took pride in everything they did. Their existence mattered.

But as they grew older, their memories faded, and so did our memories of them. We don't know how they lived, how important they were or what a great impact their lives have had on so many.

They *feel* forgotten because many times they *are* forgotten.

Please don't get me wrong. I'm not blaming anyone in particular for this devaluing of the elderly. I think we're all to blame in some way for what has happened to our Senior Citizens in our culture.

No doubt, their care-givers and families do the best they can, but apparently, a great number of our Seniors feel helpless, useless and hopeless, which, in my opinion, is the recipe for suicide. When the elderly die, we don't automatically assume they took their own lives. Honestly, I never thought about it before I found the above statistic while writing this book.

The Solution?

Let's visit with our elders. Let's pay attention to them and give them the respect and time that they deserve. If you think about it, their toil and hard work built the very towns we live in today. **We needed them when we were growing up, and now our elders need us as they are growing old.**

Regardless of the ages of our fellow human beings, it's incumbent upon each of us to care about one another. *You don't have to be crazy to consider suicide, you just have to be desperate.* Desperation can be cured. Loneliness can be cured. It just takes a little time and a relationship with others, showing people that they still matter and that they aren't forgotten. A kind word to the cashier, a compliment to the wait staff, spending some time listening to an elderly person, or a smile to a child; a little kindness goes a long way. What do you say we go out of our way and show some kindness today? It might help someone to *just hold on*.

"I'm a Christian, But I Still Get Suicidal Thoughts"

Actually, just so you know, Christians are still human. We still have thoughts and experiences. We still make bad decisions and we still do dumb things at times.

Whether you're a Christian or not, all humans share the same enemy of our souls and that is the devil. This devil is the one who plants all manner of evil thoughts in our heads.

NOTE: I think it's important to mention here that the devil CANNOT read our minds.

The Scripture is clear that satan is a created (fallen) angel. The devil is not God. Only God is all-knowing, everywhere-present, and all-powerful.

That may be a revelation to some. The devil can plant ideas and thoughts, which is what we're talking about here, but he can't hear what you're thinking. So, if you're going to battle him, it will have to be out loud using Jesus' name and the truths found in Scripture.

Having said that, it's good to be honest about these things. Sometimes Christians have bad thoughts, but it's really not the thought that's troubling, it's what we're doing with the thought that makes all the difference.

We are told in **2 Corinthians 10 verses 3-5** that we are in a spiritual battle, and we need to control our own thoughts. *"For though we walk in the flesh, we do not war according to the flesh, for the weapons of our warfare are not of the flesh, but divinely powerful for the destruction of fortresses. We are destroying speculations and every lofty thing raised up against the knowledge of God, and we are taking every thought captive to the obedience of Christ...."*

Every battle any of us will ever face starts in the mind. What we are thinking about will ultimately determine our direction and our actions. Still, while everyone has to fight this battle, the Christian is spiritually equipped to fight on a whole different level.

Ephesians 6:10-11, 13 tells us that we have certain spiritual weapons now at our disposal. *"Finally, be strong in the Lord and in the strength of His might. Put on the full armor of God, so that you will be able to*

*stand firm against the schemes of the devil." "Therefore,
take up the full armor of God, so that you will be able
to resist in the evil day, and having done everything, to
stand firm."*

Nothing about this life is easy. However, the spiritual
battle is winnable when we have our armor on, we're
clothed in the Lord Jesus Christ **(Romans 13:14)**, and
we remember to fix our eyes on Jesus, Who is the author
and finisher of our faith **(Hebrews 12:2)**.

*Of course, you're not a horrible Christian for having
suicidal thoughts, but you need to know that God has
given us the tools to overcome them.*

My Personal Counselor

After decades as a Christian, I still get down sometimes. I do. But I've noticed over the years that I don't
stay down as long, or go down as deep as I used to go. In
my continuing growth as a Christian, I have begun to see
God as my Counselor. In **Isaiah 9:6**, the Bible describes
Jesus as a *"...wonderful Counselor...."* When He left
the earth, Jesus gave His followers the Holy Spirit Who
is called, "the Spirit of Truth," and "the Comforter." One
of the absolute necessities of effective counseling is the
idea that the one being counseled would be truthful with
the counselor. I have seen over the past few years that
when I am completely honest with God about my sin and

what's going on inside of me, I can identify my problems and overcome them much faster. Jesus said that the Holy Spirit would be with us and IN us. So, that means we have a built-in counselor. I have grown leaps and bounds by allowing my Counselor to lead me into all truth, and it all starts with prayer.

How I Cope

The first thing I do is pray (*If it's a care, it's a prayer* [11]). In complete honesty with God, I tell Him exactly what my problem is, and I ask for strength, wisdom and help.

I also confess my sins, and I'm quiet as I ask God to search my heart for any wicked ways. If I have unforgiveness or bitterness towards another person, it's no wonder I'm depressed. Remember the Lord's Prayer, "... *forgive us as we forgive those who trespass against us...*" (**Matthew 6:12**) We're told to forgive people, not because God is cruel and unrealistic, but because He knows that unforgiveness will torture us, and giving forgiveness will set us free.

Going to the Word of God (the Bible), I remind myself of Who God really is. One of my favorite passages of Scripture that the Lord has used as a spiritual life preserver for me is **Lamentations 3:21-23**, *"This I recall to my mind, therefore I have hope. The LORD'S* *lovingkindnesses indeed never cease, for His compassions never fail. They are new every morning; great is Your faithfulness."*

What happens as I recall the faithfulness of God? I have hope. Hope rises up in me as I remember the Lord's faithfulness to me and His love for me. Over the years, the Bible has become a solid foundation for me to stand on. I find a lot of strength in memorizing whole chunks of the Word of God. I don't understand everything, but as I fill myself up with the Truth, the Truth can do its work of renewing my mind and transforming my life. **(Romans 12:1-2)**

Sometimes I call a friend. We need each other, Christian or not. When the first human was created, God said, *"It is not good for man to be alone."* One of the greatest strategies of the devil is to isolate us. Just like a predator with its prey, he will try to get us away from the others and after a while, without the protection of our fellow human beings, eventually we become weak. When we are weak, he comes in for the kill. I am not too proud to call on my friends to help me.

Whether it's through praying together, or going out to eat, playing a board game, or going to Church, the answer is to get around positive people. Without exception, I always feel better when I've spent some time with God's people.

And sometimes, when I'm having an especially lonely day, I will go to bed early. That's right. *Sleep is sometimes the best prescription we can give to ourselves.* Inevitably, when I wake up in the morning, I find God's new mercies, and a fresh trust in God to meet head-on the challenges of a brand new day.

Closing Thoughts

What's God Got to Do with It?

Everything, actually. God's got everything to do with all of this. Those weapons and tools and coping mechanisms that I wrote about in the last part — yeah — they aren't given to just anyone. They are only offered as a package deal with Jesus. He is the only hope any of us really have.

Maybe you're not convinced that God has anything to do with anyone's transformation. That's fine, but how do you explain all of the changes that have happened to me over the past thirty years? Was it my giant, intelligent brain that took me from despair to this unspeakable joy and contentment that I live in almost 24/7?

Did I pull myself up by my own bootstraps? Was it raw, human determination and my iron will that made me decide to live? Is that how I resisted the drive to kill myself? No, it wasn't any of those things. Even if I could have changed my life for a season, I could not have maintained that change for these many years. The fact is, before I met God, I tried numerous times to change, but I failed every time. In the end, it was Jesus alone Who saved me and Jesus alone who continues to transform me.

So, I'm sharing my own experience, my own story to tell you this truth because no one can argue with my story. *It's my story,* but it's not just my story. There are countless testimonies of how *God has taken our lives, our messes of hopelessness and turned them into messages of hope.* Ask any true Christian, and they will point to God as the One who rescued them out of the darkest pit.

Maybe you think you're not that bad. You're saying, *"Yeah, but I never killed anyone. I haven't done illegal drugs. I'm not a bad guy..."* And I'm sure all of that is true, but you're not perfect. None of us are. That's why we needed a perfect Savior to rescue us. I'm sure you've heard before that the Bible says, *"All have sinned."* Ok, well what does that matter to you?

It matters because the wages or paycheck for that sin is death. Hell is a real place that was originally made for the devil and his angels, not for humans (**Matthew 25:41**). Hell is where those who will pay for their own sin will go. You can believe that or not, it's your choice.

If I'm wrong, no worries for me, but if you're wrong, then there's plenty of reason for you to worry.

Don't despair. I have some good news for you! The good news is that Jesus came to pay that sin debt in full for all of mankind! But only those who *receive* the gift will be able to enjoy total forgiveness and eternal life in heaven. It gets even better. This gift is easy to receive. Just ask God to forgive you and to save you. (See "**Oh, One More Thing**" for details on how to receive this *gift*).

Of course, you don't have to believe me, but if you're still reading this, these truths have become a seeds in the soil of your soul. I pray that the Lord will water those seeds and bring you to Himself.

As we have seen in the pages of this book, we are not promised tomorrow. God is not trying to hurt you. He's trying to bring you back into relationship with Him. YOU are loved. If by no one else, you are loved by God.

What's God got to do with it? **Everything.**

Oh, One More Thing

Wherever you are, if you feel like you're in too far to be able to fight this on your own, please call on Jesus to save you. Ask Him to help you and I guarantee He will. How can I be so confident that God will come to your rescue? Well, three reasons actually. One, He helped *me* when I called out to Him in my desperation. Two, He's helped others in the same way, and three, the Bible clearly says He will help you. *"Whoever will call upon the name of the Lord will be saved."* **(Romans 10:8)**

It doesn't have to be a fancy prayer. My prayer wasn't complicated, but Jesus saved *me*. I would love to introduce you to Jesus, but you don't need me to meet Him. If you call for Him, He will come to you right now. Email me at dhaasbigd@gmail.com if you make a decision to follow Jesus. I would love to give you some material to help you in your new journey. Don't give up. Don't quit. *Just hold on.*

"...if you confess with your mouth Jesus as Lord, and believe in your heart that God raised Him from the dead, you will be saved; for with the heart a person believes, resulting in righteousness, and with the mouth he confesses, resulting in salvation." (Romans 10:9-10)

Just Hold On—A Poem

"***Just hold on*** *for one more second, just one more minute, just one more hour.*
Just hold on *for one more sunrise, one more time to open your eyes to blue skies and hope and love and the warmth of the sun.*
*If you **just hold on**, you'll have the strength and the power to rise above this sorrow,*
to come up for air and wake up tomorrow to find that because you held on your future is intact. In fact, you were always meant to make it through, you know?
Your courage is found in living, not dying. In helping, not hurting. In life and not death.
Your courage is found in taking a breath and holding on for just one more second, just one more minute, just one more hour.
Just hold on *for one more sunrise, one more time to open your eyes to blue skies*
and hope and love and the warmth of the sun.
Just let your lungs keep breathing ... and please,
just hold on." *dh*

The End?

No. I believe it can be a brand new beginning if you *just hold on.* I'm praying for you.

Shalom (peace),

Denise

How Can I Help In This Fight Against Suicide?

HELP! (The immediate crisis)

A t times we may find ourselves face to face with someone who is threatening suicide. *"Don't do it!"* or *"What are you thinking?"* may not be as helpful as we might hope for it to be. This next section is designed to avoid the "deer in the headlights" response to a suicidal person's immediate crisis by offering a (non-exhaustive) list of options. You don't have to be a trained professional to help a person in crisis. If you're willing and available, God can use you.

Even though there is no order to this list as each scenario will be different, there is absolutely one thing that all of us must do **FIRST**, and that is to **ASK GOD FOR HELP.** Please do not try anything until you've asked the Lord to help you. He may give you some really good answers based upon the fact that HE can see the heart of the person you are dealing with. Also, don't panic. Try to remain calm and non-judgmental. Trust that as you have asked God to step in, He has, and He is working on the inside of the person.

The following suggestions are not intended to take the place of professional help, nor are they rules to be followed. They are simply options to help lay people should they find themselves face to face with a person who is suicidal.

- Sit with the person until the crisis has passed. If you have to leave, find someone else who can take over for you.
- Ask the one in crisis if they have a plan. If the answer is yes, ask them to reveal it to you.
- Ask them to promise not to hurt themselves. Write a simple "contract" to this effect. Ask them to sign it.
- Hear the words the person is saying to you, but listen to their heart in the way they say it. Again, don't judge, just listen.
- Try talking to them. Talk about their kids or about those who love them. Tell them that they matter.
- Pray with them if they are willing. *(Never stop praying silently for wisdom.)*
- Walk with them, or take them for coffee. Sometimes it just helps to change the location of the person in crisis. If the outside environment

is not ideal, help to change the atmosphere by offering to *make* coffee, turn on the TV, or play a board game.

- If they are creative, ask to see or hear a project *(a painting/drawing, song, poem, etc.)* they have done or something they are currently working on.
- Talk about their future. Make a plan to meet with them for breakfast or lunch the next day or in a week. Try to give them something to look forward to.

When to call 911:

- If the person has a weapon, and you can not get it away from them or you're on the phone with someone who says they have a weapon.
- If there is no one to stay with the person in crisis.
- If the person says they have a plan to take their own life but they won't reveal it to you.
- If the person tells you that they're fine and that you can go, but you're not sure they are passed the crisis, call another person, or call 911.

Another resource to help if you are suicidal or know of someone who is: 1-888-NEED-HIM

Ways to "Cut In" (Everyday life)

I believe we can all "cut in" on this dance with suicide. Even if it's just by being kind, defending the one who's being bullied, sending that letter or email, or calling that person whom you know could use a friend. How about if we each contribute to the prevention of suicide by helping to prevent depression.

It's free to send an email. It doesn't cost anything to say some kind words to a person who's down in the dumps. Having said that, "cutting in" doesn't always stop a person from taking their own life. Still, we have to try.

Let's make it our mission to encourage everyone we meet, letting them know that there is hope. You never know, by making a simple phone call you just may be tapping on the shoulder of Suicide and "cutting in" to effectively change the dance partner from Death to Life.

A Prayer

"Jesus, please equip every single person to speak words of life to everyone we come in contact with. I believe You are the miracle worker, and so I humbly ask that no one in my area would complete the act of suicide. Not only through prevention by divine intervention, but also through the touch of human conversation and relationship. That Lord, you would put us in the right place at the right time, saying just the right words to people who need it the most and where it will make the most

difference. Please make me sensitive to every prompting, no matter how small or ridiculous or out of reach, it may seem. I want to believe You in a manner that is worthy of You, Lord. I believe that you love people more than I could possibly imagine. I am willing for You to use me to speak Your words of life, or write a letter from You, or sit with them, even if it's only for one hour. Help me, Lord. Use me for the glory of Your kingdom and as an instrument of Your grace. I pray this in the name that is above every name, Jesus."

Scriptures Used in This Book

"The Lord GOD has given Me the tongue of disciples, that I may know how to sustain the weary one with a word…." (Isaiah 50:4)

"For this reason I say to you, do not be worried about your life, as to what you will eat or what you will drink; nor for your body, as to what you will put on. Is not life more than food, and the body more than clothing? Look at the birds of the air, that they do not sow, nor reap nor gather into barns, and yet your heavenly Father feeds them. Are you not worth much more than they? And who of you by being worried can add a single hour to his life?" (Matthew 6:25-27)

"My heavenly Father will also do the same to you, if each of you does not forgive his brother from your heart.'" (Matthew 18:32-35)

"Forgive them Father for they know not what they do." (Luke 23:24)

"Death and life are in the power of the tongue, and those who love it will eat its fruit." (Proverbs 18:21)

"When I kept silent about my sin, my body wasted away through my groaning all day long. For day and night Your hand was heavy upon me; my vitality was drained away as with the fever heat of summer." (Psalm 32: 3,4)

"The thief comes only to steal and kill and destroy..."

"I came that they may have life, and have it abundantly." (John 10:10)

"Even though I walk through the valley of the shadow of death, I will fear no evil for Thou art with me; Thy rod and Thy staff, they comfort me." (Psalm 23:4)

"Finally, be strong in the Lord and in the strength of His might. Put on the full armor of God, so that you will be able to stand firm against the schemes of the devil." *"Therefore, take up the full armor of God, so that you will be able to resist in the evil day, and having done everything, to stand firm."* (Ephesians 6:10-11, 13)

"...forgive us as we forgive those who trespass against us..." (Matthew 6:12)

"This I recall to my mind, therefore I have hope. The LORD'S lovingkindnesses indeed never cease, for His compassions never fail. They are new every morning; great is Your faithfulness." (Lamentations 3:21-23)

"Whoever will call upon the name of the Lord will be saved." (Romans 10:8)

"...if you confess with your mouth Jesus as Lord, and believe in your heart that God raised Him from the dead, you will be saved; for with the heart a person believes, resulting in righteousness, and with the mouth he confesses, resulting in salvation." (Romans 10:9-10))

References/sources:

1. USA suicide 2006 Official final data: JL McIntosh for the American Association of Suicidology 2009. Many figures there taken from Reducing Suicide: a national imperative, Goldsmith SK, Pellmar TC, Kleinman AM, Bunney WE, editors. https://en.wikipedia.org/wiki/Suicide_attempt#cite_note-2
2. The Skyway Bridge is one of the most used bridges for suicide in the Nation. http://www.tampabay.com/news/publicsafety/woman-43-survives-jump-from-top-of-sunshine-skyway-bridge/830880
3. Prison dog programs: Article by REBECCA L. RHOADES https://www.petfinder.com/animal-shelters-and-rescues/volunteering-with-dogs/prison-dog-programs/

4. Dehydration: http://www.mayoclinic.org/diseases-conditions/dehydration/basics/symptoms/con-20030056
5. Water benefits: http://water.usgs.gov/edu/propertyyou.html
6. Suicide is second leading cause of death in 15-24yr olds http://www.cdc.gov/ViolencePrevention/pdf/Suicide-DataSheet-a.pdf
7. 1 out of every 4 attempted suicides in the elderly ends in death. http://www.save.org/index.cfm?fuseaction=home.viewPage&page_id=705D5DF4-055B-F1EC-3F66462866FCB4E6
8. http://www.livestrong.com/article/22590-effects-exercise-serotonin-levels/ The National Institute for Health and Clinical Excellence, of the United Kingdom, exercise increases brain serotonin function in humans. A study published in Neuropsychopharmacology.
9. Thyroid gland http://www.endocrineweb.com/conditions/thyroid-nodules/thyroid-gland-controls-bodys-metabolism-how-it-works-symptoms-hyperthyroid
10. "If it's a care, it's a prayer!" Denise Haas
11. Toby Mac http://www.tobymac.com/
12. Big D & the Good News Blues http://www.bigdblues.com

About the Author

Denise Haas, aka Big D is a suicide attempt survivor. In her early years, Denise was in deep despair, and had an obsession with death. Today, she is overflowing with hope and living life to the fullest.

Photo cred: Erica Haas

She is a wife, a mother, mother-in-law, a grandma, friend, minister, musician, writer, and a passionate follower of Jesus. Her life's goal is to be a blessing to others—helping in every way possible to bring hope to those who are lost in the darkness.

Denise currently resides in the **Upper Peninsula of Michigan** with her husband, one cat, and her Wiener-Poo puppy.

You can find out more about Denise within the pages of this book in the "Note To Self" section, find her on Facebook (Denise Haas), or go to her website, bigdblues.com.

CPSIA information can be obtained
at www.ICGtesting.com
Printed in the USA
FFOW05n0641011116

9 781498 487665